christmas family gatherings

•••

W9-CDL-770

christmas family gatherings

• • •

recipes and ideas for celebrating with people you love

by donata maggipinto

•

photographs

by france ruffenach

CHRONICLE BOOKS

SAN FRANCISCO

Text copyright © 2003 by Donata Maggipinto.
Photographs copyright © 2003 by France Ruffenach.
All rights reserved. No part of this book may
be reproduced in any form without written
permission from the publisher.

Library of Congress Cataloging-in-Publication Data:
Maggipinto, Donata.
    Christmas family gatherings : recipes and ideas
for celebrating with people you love / by Donata
Maggipinto; photographs by France Ruffenach.
        p. cm.
    ISBN 0-8118-4018-2
1. Christmas cookery. 2. Christmas decorations.
I. Title.
    TX739.2.C45 M34 2003
    641.5'68—dc21
        2002154277

Manufactured in China.

Designed by Lori Barra, TonBo designs
Design Assistant: Jan Martí, Command Z
Prop styling by Aaron Hom
Food styling by Diane Scott Gsell
Assistant Food Stylist: Diane Huntsinger

The photographer wishes to thank Donata and Reyn,
Courtney Reeser, Vanessa Dina, Leslie Jonath,
Lori Barra, Aaron Hom, Diane Scott Gsell,
Diane Huntsinger, Frank Gaglione, Brandon
McGanty, and Sara Schneider.

Distributed in Canada by Raincoast Books
9050 Shaughnessy Street
Vancouver, British Columbia V6P 6E5

10 9 8 7 6 5 4 3 2 1

Chronicle Books LLC
85 Second Street
San Francisco, California 94105

www.chroniclebooks.com

Callebaut is a registered trademark of Chocolaterie Bernard
Callebaut. Hersey's Chocolate Kisses is a registered trademark of
the Hershey Foods Corporation. M&M's candy is a registered
trademark of Mars, Inc. Popsicle is a registered trademark of
Good Humor-Breyers Ice Cream. Red Hots candy is a registered
trademark of Ferrara Pan Candy Co., Inc. Scotch Tape is a
registered trademark of Minnesota Mining and Manufacturing
Company. Styrofoam is a registered trademark of the Dow
Chemical Company. Tabasco is a registered trademark of
McIlhenny Co. Tootsie Pop is a registered trademark of Tootsie
Roll Industries, Inc. Twizzlers candy is a registered trademark
of the Hershey Foods Corporation. Valrhona chocolate is a
registered trademark of Valrhona S.A. Worcestershire Sauce is
a registered trademark of HP Foods, Ltd.

With Appreciation

Thanks to everyone at Chronicle Books. To my editor, Leslie Jonath, for her
unbridled enthusiasm, able guidance, and patience. To Lisa Campbell for her
organizational fortitude. To Vanessa Dina, for her creative expertise, and to
Lori Barra, for her design. I am also grateful to Sharon Silva, Jan Hughes,
Doug Ogan, Steve Kim, and everybody else who worked behind the scenes on
behalf of my book.

I owe heartfelt gratitude to my wonderful photography team. Merci to France
Ruffenach for her creativity and technical expertise; each photo is a jewel. Many
thanks to Aaron Hom, who interepreted my ideas with style and finesse. A big
thank-you to Diane Gsell for her special blend of practicality and artistic expression
with both food and crafts. To Diane Huntsinger for excellent kitchen assistance,
and to Frank Gaglione, for his photographic support. And a sugar-kissed thank-you
to my adorable cookie-decorating models, Nicolas and Gabriela Aparicio, and
Briggs Woolley.

Thanks to Angela Miller, for her unerring support. Thanks to everyone at the
Today show: Betsy Alexander, Dee Dee Thomas, Katie (gracias!), Matt, Ann, and Al.

I sincerely thank Amanda Haas for her thorough recipe testing and enthusiasm.
A big hug to Chuck Williams, who inspires me every day. Kisses to Chris Bridge and
Sandy Peterson, who share my love for food and entertaining (and laughing) on a
daily basis. To Amanda Marcus, a modern-day Mame, for her perpetual optimism
and sense of fun. To Gates McKibbin for shining the light.

Finally, this book could never have been written without the people who define
Christmas for me. Love and thanks to Mom and Dad, who took the holiday
traditions they knew in their respective Irish and Italian families and melded them
into a joyous celebration that my sisters and I reveled in each year (we still do).
Hugs and kisses to my sisters, Deidre, Diane, and Dina. There's nothing like
throwing tinsel on the tree, giggling through midnight mass, and eating too many
Christmas Eve cannoli to seal a lifelong holiday bond. *Buon Natale!*

To the Reeser family for sharing their West Coast holiday traditions and for playing
such a loving role in our Christmas rituals today. And to our beloved friends,
family in every way, who bring love and light into our home each Christmas Eve.
Our holiday just wouldn't be the same without Neal, Jeff, Susie, Paul, and Jackson.

And to my husband, Courtney, my stepson, Chance, and my son, Reyn, who make
every day Christmas for me. I love you.

In memory of my Aunt Ceil,
who lived Christmas every day.
"Isn't that wild?"

·

And for Courtney, Chance, and Reyn
with love.

contents

It's a given. As soon as I hear the first Christmas song of the season I become weepy—in the happiest way possible. The old-fashioned tune "Have Yourself a Merry Little Christmas," with its happy dictum "let your heart be light" and its wish for "faithful friends who are dear to us, gather near to us," particularly moves me. How perfect, then, that these words so aptly describe what is at the heart of *Christmas Family Gatherings*.

This book captures the simple pleasures that infuse Christmas with magic and meaning. For me, that's focusing on what matters most: Spending time with family and friends in a comfortable home, cooking festive foods and enjoying them with others in a beautiful setting, and sharing time-honored holiday traditions, while creating new ones.

Christmas Family Gatherings is devoted to simple, delicious, and beautiful holiday pleasures to be shared with family and friends. From complete menus for holiday parties and easy decorating tips for your home to how-tos for clever gifts, the ideas that fill the following pages are designed to help you connect with those you love during the holidays. And because children are the heart of the holidays for so many of us, all the activities and parties in *Christmas Family Gatherings* are kid-friendly, too.

For many people, Christmas is about the grand gesture—spending days and nights in frenzied cooking and decorating, enduring crowds to buy piles of gifts, and attending to a calendar chock-full of obligations. The funny thing is, at the end of all the huzzah and hurrah, many of us are exhausted rather than exhilarated.

Here's one secret to ease the exhaustion: smaller is better. No kidding. It's the small gestures and the little details that elevate everyday moments into celebrations. Why not use the holiday china for a weeknight supper? Prepare hot cocoa from scratch? Or make an evening ritual out of opening the Christmas cards that arrived in the day's mail?

At the core of *Christmas Family Gatherings* are age-old traditions, updated for today's families. Holiday customs and rituals, those activities we engage in just once a year, are particularly significant for children. They give a sure rhythm to the season and provide something certain for them to look forward to each December. For children (and for adults, too), rituals that are re-enacted annually—the same cookies baked and decorated, the same ornaments unwrapped and hung on the tree, the same guests around the Christmas table—build on the memories of Christmases past, enriching their sense of family and strengthening their connections with others.

Indeed, family enlivens Christmas. Today, family transcends the sociological "nuclear family" of 2 parents and 2.5 kids (where did that come from?) to include childless couples, same-sex partners, roommates, and work colleagues. Whether related through blood or through the accrual of shared experiences, family is defined by a connection rooted in love.

When diverse families and friends come together, traditions and rituals converge. You don't have to do them all, just the ones that have meaning for you. And by all means, create your own customs, too. Peppermint-stick ice cream for breakfast? Why not!

For *Christmas Family Gatherings*, I have created six holiday parties, complete with menus and style ideas. The recipes are simple, straightforward, and time-efficient, and the decorating and craft ideas are both imaginative and easy to complete. From a casual snowy day fondue lunch (page 156) and a girlfriends' gift-wrapping party (page 140) to an afternoon cookie-decorating party for the children (page 122) to a magical white Christmas Eve dinner (page 44) that concludes with a snowman cake (page 57), you will find recipes and ideas to complement your own family's traditions.

Remember to find ways to involve your children in the kitchen and at the craft table. They're inherently creative and love to be included. Invite them to measure, mix, and decorate. Encourage them to join you in making Christmas cards, place cards, and adornments, too. As you spend time with them, you will discover ample opportunities to relate stories of your childhood holidays, or to explain the tradition that is at the root of the activity you are sharing.

Much of the pleasure and satisfaction we receive from the holidays comes from giving to others, so I've also included a section called Holiday Notions (page 12) that offers quick and easy ideas for making and giving gifts. Homemade gifts are special because you put your heart and your hands into making them. Involving your children in assembling the gifts will not only please them, but will also teach them that doing something for others is a gratifying experience. Among these seasonal notions are such edible gifts as chocolate stars (page 17), and such deliciously aromatic tokens as a Christmas potpourri (page 33).

Now that you know what *Christmas Family Gatherings* is, let me tell you what it is not. It is not a book full of impossible expectations that shout, "More is better!" I bid you: do not fall into the perfection trap. Perfection is a goal that brings with it only two certainties: it can never be attained and it will throw you into the depths of frustration and exhaustion. There is no such thing as a "perfect" Christmas. Instead, strive for a satisfying one—one that speaks to you on the deepest level because it is made up of family and friends and foods and activities that matter to you.

So here's my mantra for this holiday (are you with me?): Focus on the meaningful. Do less. Enjoy your holiday more. Celebrate Christmas in your own wonderful way with people you love—and have fun while you do.

Have yourself a merry little Christmas. *Donata*

Holiday Notions

Homemade Gifts and Decorations That Celebrate the Season

Today, Christmas is often defined by a surfeit of gifts, but in Victorian times, it was typified by time spent relaxing with family and friends. Small seasonal gifts called "holiday notions" were exchanged. These items were usually homemade, because the Victorians believed that the most thoughtful holiday gesture was the act of doing on behalf of another.

This section presents more than twenty simple ideas that commemorate the season in straightforward and pleasing ways, all of them based on longstanding holiday traditions that I have updated here. They offer the opportunity to connect with family and friends by making the projects together, and they serve as thoughtful gestures when you share them with others.

hot cocoa kit

Hot cocoa is a Christmas tradition in Austria. In fact, the Austrians have elevated cocoa making to an art and an occasion. A day of Christmas shopping in Vienna would be incomplete without a stop at Demel, the city's turn-of-the-century mirrored and marbled café, for a cup of Schokolade mit Schlag *(hot cocoa with whipped cream).*

This easy-to-make hot cocoa mix celebrates that Austrian tradition. It also is fun to create a gift kit with the mix as the centerpiece. Package it in a pretty gift box lined with tissue. Include Hershey Kisses—they further sweeten and deepen the chocolate flavor—and marshmallows for dropping into the cocoa, if you wish.

Spice-Kissed Hot Cocoa Mix

FOR 8 CUPS

1/3 cup best-quality unsweetened cocoa powder

1/4 cup superfine sugar

1 whole star anise

2 cinnamon sticks, each about 3 inches long

Mix together all ingredients. Place in a tin or jar that seals securely. Add a recipe card with the following directions:

Hot Cocoa

8 cups whole milk	8 Hershey Kisses (optional)
Spice-Kissed Hot Cocoa Mix	marshmallows (optional)

In a heavy saucepan over low heat, bring 1 cup of the milk to a simmer. Stir in the cocoa mix. Mix until well blended. Add the remaining 7 cups milk and bring back to a simmer.

Remove the star anise and the cinnamon sticks and discard. Serve hot, along with the Hershey Kisses and marshmallows, if desired.

candied orange peel

Candied fruits embellish many Christmas breads, from the Santa Lucia bun in Sweden to panettone in Italy to stollen in Germany. These sweet breads hark back to a time when fruits, and especially exotic fruits like citrus, were expensive and only used to commemorate special days. Candied orange peel adds bright flavor to cookies, cakes, and muffins, too. On its own it makes a delicious snack, an elegant accompaniment to after-dinner coffee, or a thoughtful gift.

MAKES 2 TO 3 CUPS

3 oranges, preferably organic
1/2 cup water, plus more for cooking
1 cup sugar, plus more to coat
1 1/2 tablespoons corn syrup

Scrub and rinse the oranges well, then dry. Cut a slice off the top and bottom of each orange. Score the oranges vertically in quarters and remove the peel. Cut the peel lengthwise into 1/4 inch-wide strips. (Reserve the orange flesh for another use.)

Place the orange peel in a heavy saucepan and cover with cold water. Bring to a boil over high heat, reduce the heat to low, and simmer, uncovered, for 45 minutes. Drain. Put the peel in a bowl, cover with cold water, and let stand for at least 1 hour or up to overnight. Drain the orange peel and reserve.

In the same saucepan, combine the 1/2 cup water, the 1 cup sugar, and the corn syrup and stir to combine. Place over medium heat and bring to a boil, stirring to dissolve the sugar. Add the orange peel, reduce the heat to low, and simmer, stirring occasionally, until the peel has almost completely absorbed the syrup, about 1 hour.

Set a cooling rack on a large piece of waxed paper. Using a slotted spoon, transfer the orange peel to the cooling rack. Let cool for 1 to 2 hours.

Cover the bottom of a shallow bowl with sugar. Working in batches, roll the orange peel in the sugar to coat each strip evenly. Store in an airtight container in a cool, dry place for up to 1 month or in the freezer for up to 3 months.

chocolate stars

From the top of the Christmas tree to the lights twinkling on its branches, stars are everywhere at Christmastime. The three wise men are said to have relied on a star to navigate their way to Bethlehem. Some people believe that Santa depends on the stars, too, as he soars through the Christmas Eve sky.

Easy to make and pretty to behold, these chocolate stars deliciously commemorate the Christmas symbol. If you're giving a dinner party, set a star at each person's place. Or tuck a few stars into waxed-paper bags, fold over the tops, and seal with Christmas stickers—ready to bestow on holiday visitors at a moment's notice.

MAKES ABOUT 12 TWO-INCH STARS

8 ounces bittersweet chocolate, chopped
candy sprinkles or confetti (optional)
gold leaf (optional)
silver dragées (optional)
Candied Orange Peel (facing page), chopped (optional)

Place the chocolate in the top of a double boiler set over barely simmering water. Heat, stirring gently, until melted, then remove from the heat. Let the chocolate cool until it is thick enough to pipe (85°F to 90°F on a candy thermometer).

While the chocolate is cooling, using a star template about 2 inches wide, trace stars onto a sheet of waxed paper. When the chocolate is cool enough to pipe, spoon it into a pastry bag fitted with a small star icing tip and pipe it onto the waxed paper, following the star outlines. It is not necessary to fill in the star entirely. Let the chocolate set for about 5 minutes.

If you like, decorate the stars with candy sprinkles or confetti, gold leaf, silver dragées, and orange peel, then gently press the decorations onto the chocolate so they adhere. Let the chocolate cool completely. Cover and store at room temperature for up to 1 month.

santa lollipops

The happiest of all Christmas icons, Santa deserves a sweet portrayal. He receives it in the form of these lollipops. Children will enjoy decorating Santa's face, but they may need assistance from an adult when cutting and affixing Santa's red-and-white hat to the lollipop. If you're on the list to bring holiday treats to your child's school, these jolly lollies are just the ticket. Wrapped in cellophane, they are cheerful stocking stuffers. They also make cute party favors for the Just-for-Kids Cookie Decorating Party (page 122).

FOR EACH LOLLIPOP, YOU WILL NEED:

* 1 small sheet red construction paper
* 3-inch round cookie cutter or other template
* pencil
* scissors
* 1 globe lollipop such as a Tootsie Pop, 1¹/₂ to 2 inches in diameter
* craft glue or Scotch tape
* 1 small cotton ball
* decorative icing pens, white plus other colors of choice
* short, narrow glass such as a juice glass, or Styrofoam block

Lay the red construction paper on a work surface and, using the cookie cutter or other template and the pencil, trace a circle. Cut out the circle with the scissors, then cut the circle in half. Form one half circle into a cone hat to fit Santa's head (the lollipop) and use glue or tape to secure the ends. Glue or tape the cotton ball to the top of the hat. (The extra half circle can be used for making a second Santa.)

Paint the bottom edges of Santa's hat with the white icing pens and gently set it on Santa's head (the lollipop). Some of the icing will seep through to form a white rim on Santa's hat.

Use the remaining decorative icing pens to paint Santa's beard, eyes, nose, and mouth on the lollipop. Gently set the lollipop upright in the glass or insert the stick in the Styrofoam block. Let stand for 1 hour to set.

salt dough ornaments

No doubt you learned this recipe in childhood. Remember how much fun it was? Now's the time to share it with your own children. Use this dough to make a parade of Santas, a constellation of stars, or a procession of angels. Line them up on your fireplace mantel or along the windowsill in your child's bedroom, or give them to a friend.

MAKES ABOUT 2 DOZEN ORNAMENTS, DEPENDING ON SIZE

4 cups all-purpose flour

1 cup salt

1 1/2 cups water

cookie stamp(s) or cookie cutter(s), about 3 inches across, in shape(s) of choice

wooden skewer

paintbrush

tempera paints in colors of choice

glitter (optional)

fishing line or ribbon

Preheat the oven to 300°F.

In a large bowl, stir together the flour, salt, and water. Turn out onto a lightly floured work surface and knead until a stiff dough forms. If the mixture cracks when pinched, add a bit more water. The mixture should be smooth.

Pinch golf-ball-size bits from the dough and roll or pat flat. Use the cookie stamps or cutters to make the ornaments. With a wooden skewer, punch a hole near the top of each cutout.

Transfer the cutouts to baking sheets, spacing the cutouts about 1 inch apart. Bake until set (they will feel firm to the touch), 1 to 1 1/2 hours. Remove from the oven and transfer the cutouts to racks. Let dry at room temperature for 3 days. Paint with tempera paints. If using glitter, sprinkle it onto the cutouts while the paint is still wet.

When the cutouts are dry, cut fishing line or ribbon into desired lengths. Thread a piece through the hole at the top of each cutout and tie securely, forming a loop for hanging.

the birds' christmas tree

On Christmas Day in Scandinavian countries, a sheaf of wheat is hung outside for the birds to enjoy. It is believed that showing kindness to animals will bring prosperity in the new year. When I was a child, my classmates and I made these birdseed-and-suet balls in school and brought them home as gifts for our parents. Whether you wrap the balls in cellophane and give them away to friends or keep them for your own garden, hungry birds will also enjoy this Christmas treat. Ask your butcher to special-order the suet if he or she does not regularly have it on hand.

1/2 cup finely chopped nuts	3 cups (about 1 pound) beef suet
1/2 cup finely chopped raisins	wooden skewer
1 1/2 cups seed for wild birds	twine
1/2 cup rolled oats	darning needle

In a large bowl, combine the nuts, raisins, birdseed, and rolled oats; reserve.

In a saucepan over medium-low heat, melt the suet. While stirring with a wooden spoon, pour enough of the melted suet into the birdseed mixture, to form a stiff paste. Let stand just until cool enough to handle, about 5 minutes.

On a work surface, using your hands, mold the mixture into balls of various sizes. With the wooden skewer, make a hole through the center of each ball from top to bottom. Select a ball. Thread the twine through the darning needle so you have two pieces of equal length. The doubled length should be about 6 inches longer than the diameter of the ball. Thread the twine, from bottom to top, through the hole, leaving 3 inches of twine at each end. There should be a loop at the top of the ball and two loose pieces at the bottom. Cut the twine at the top of the ball to remove the needle, then tie it to remake a loop. Tie the loose pieces at the bottom into a knot that rests against the ball. Let cool completely. Repeat with the remaining balls. Hang the suet balls on tree branches outdoors. (Don't tell the neighborhood cat.)

the welcoming candle

In Colonial times in New England, candles were placed in the front windows of houses as a sign to passersby that warmth, shelter, and hospitality could be found inside.

To create your own welcoming candle, decorate a pillar candle with evergreen and berries, beads, or tiny pinecones—whatever strikes your fancy. Affix the decorations with craft glue or double-sided tape, or simply arrange them around the base of the candle. Place the candle in the window to welcome your family and holiday guests. Choose a scented candle such as pine or bayberry, and the aroma of the holidays will float through your home as the candle glows in your window.

To turn this tradition into a gift, make a welcoming candle kit. Using double-sided tape or craft glue, attach silver dragées or beads to a clear glass votive candleholder. Place the votive candleholder in a wooden box along with scented votive candles and matches. Decorate the matchbox, too. Include a cranberry bobeche (page 97), or wax catcher, as a fresh and useful token of the holiday season. Using a waterproof felt-tip pen, such as a Sharpie, write the story of the welcoming candle tradition on the outside of the box. Finish the package with a velvet ribbon.

winter wind bath salts

A warm bath infused with the invigorating scents of pine, cedar, and eucalyptus will energize even the most tired holiday shopper—just like a winter wind.

Place 2 cups Epsom salts in a medium bowl. Add 1 or 2 drops each of pine, cedar and eucalyptus essential oils (available in craft stores or aromatherapy shops), or choose a single scent. Add a few small pine sprigs. Mix well. Transfer the salts to one or more tightly closed jars or well-tied cellophane bags and let stand for at least 2 weeks to allow time for the oils to scent the salts. Include a tag instructing the recipient to place a few tablespoons of the bath salts under the faucet when the bath is drawn.

These bath salts are the perfect party favor for the Gift Wrapping Get-Together (page 140).

snow-kissed votives

Before electricity was discovered, people depended upon candles for both light and heat during the winter solstice. Romans lit candles during this time to encourage the sun to shine again. Today, candles continue to play a significant role in our holiday observances, from religious ceremonies such as Advent and Candlemas to the more secular lighting of our homes.

Nobody can have enough candles for Christmas. These little votives are extra special because they're snow-kissed!

To make the votives, purchase self-adhesive Christmas shapes or cut out your own from self-adhesive paper. Apply to the clean and dry exterior surface of clear glass votive candleholders.

Cover a work surface with newspaper. Have ready silver or opaque white glitter. Spray the candleholders with spray adhesive (available in craft stores) and apply the glitter immediately. Let dry according to directions on the spray adhesive can, then remove the adhesive paper.

Nestle votive candles in the holders, light them, and watch them glow. They take on a magical aura when nestled among pine boughs on a fireplace mantel, and they wink warmly when set on a windowsill or down the length of a dining table. They also make festive decorations for the buffet in the Tree-Trimming Open House (page 100).

miniature boxwood
doorbell wreath

There's nothing like the tinkling of bells to herald "Christmas is here!" In fact, until the late nineteenth century, bell-ringing ceremonies commonly heralded the holiday season throughout the United States.

I like to hang bells on all the doorknobs in our house so we are guaranteed to hear Christmas ringing every day, all day. A nice way to dress up the bells is to suspend them on small boxwood wreaths. Although I make the wreaths with fresh boxwood, you can also use artificial boxwood (available in floral-supply and craft stores), which will let you use your doorbell wreath for years to come.

To make the wreath, form a 12-inch length of boxwood into a circle and secure it with florist's wire. (Alternatively, use shorter lengths of boxwood and link them into a circle with florist's wire.) Using more florist's wire, attach miniature bells (available in craft stores) and a bow to the wreath. Hang on the nearest doorknob. Be happy.

thumbprint cards

The Christmas card was invented in London in the mid-1800s by John Calcott Horsely. More than a simple greeting, the card was intended to be a gift that the recipient would display in his or her home throughout the year. The first Christmas card depicted a family enjoying a holiday feast, and the cards were delivered when most people were enjoying just such a repast—on Christmas Day!

This year, instead of purchasing cards or penning the holiday letter, why not send your family's thumbprints? Using a rubber-stamp ink pad, press your thumb into the ink and then onto the front of a plain white card. Then transform the thumbprints into snowmen, reindeer, elves, and other holiday motifs with felt-tip markers or colored pencils. For example, three thumbprints, one on top of the other, can become a jolly snowman. One small thumbprint (head) next to a larger one (body) can become a reindeer.

Inside the card, write a holiday greeting. Since each card is a one-of-a-kind work of art, you can tailor the message to the recipient. Whimsical and clever, the cards are guaranteed to make people smile.

Incidentally, thumbprint cards make wonderful gift tags or place cards for a holiday dinner party.

our house christmas cards

One year, a friend sent this holiday card. It's a clever way to express Christmas wishes "from our house to yours."

To make the card, select a 4-by-6-inch family photo and make copies of it (as many copies as you will need cards). If you want to be really literal, ask a friend to take your family photo in the front doorway.

Using card stock in the color of your choice, fold it in half to measure 5 by 7 inches. You will have 4 panels: front, inside front, inside back, and back. Using construction paper, a ruler, and a pencil, draw a roof shape to fit one end of the card, then cut it out with scissors. Using craft glue, attach the roof to the inside back of the card so you can see it from the front. Cut out a chimney and glue it onto the roof. Draw a door on the front of the card, a bit smaller than your photo. Using scissors or an X-acto knife, cut out the door, leaving the left edge intact so the door can open and close. (Make sure you cut through only the front panel of the card.) Tape or glue the photo in place inside the card so your family is looking through the front door, then glue the outside edges of the card—not the door!—closed. On the back of the card, write a holiday greeting.

You can find envelopes to fit your card at stationery or office-supply shops.

custom-made rubber stamp

Years ago, Christmas greetings were personalized with sealing-wax stamps on the envelopes.
A rubber stamp is easier to use and conveys the same idea.

You can make your own rubber stamp for cards, stationery, and notepads. For each stamp, you will need a white-gum artist's eraser, found in art-supply or craft stores. Using a cookie cutter, press it into the eraser as far you can. With a meat pounder, hammer it through the eraser. Alternatively, wear a pair of thick-soled shoes and stand on the cutter until it goes through the eraser.

Now, using an ink pad in the color of your choice, press the rubber stamp into the ink and then onto cards or stationery. You can use holiday-themed rubber stamps to make your own gift wrap, too. When you're using the rubber stamp for multiple applications, insert a pushpin into the back of the stamp for a handle.

Create a gift of a stationery kit by packaging the rubber stamp with plain note cards, an ink pad, and postal stamps. Arrange the kit items in a small, colorful plastic index card box (available in office-supply stores) and finish the kit with ribbon. The box not only presents your gift cleverly, but also provides a practical storage solution for the kit, too.

ribbon christmas stocking

One of the first legends about Saint Nicholas takes place in western Turkey, purportedly his birthplace. Late at night, he visited the homes of needy children and threw gold coins down their chimneys. The coins often landed in the stockings that were hung on the fireplace mantel to dry—hence, the Christmas stocking tradition.

To make a ribbon stocking, you will need a store-bought Christmas stocking with a wide, plain cuff. Decorate the cuff with ribbons and trim such as rickrack, attaching them with fabric glue. Don't be afraid to break out of the expected red and green motif. Let your imagination inspire you. Pink! Purple! Polka dots! Finish the stocking with ribbon streamers and a loop: Gather six to twelve ribbons in lengths at least twice as long as the stocking. Fold the ribbons in half and pinch them together to create a 2-inch loop at the top. Stitch the bottom of the loop (where you pinched it) onto one side of the cuff so the stocking can hang.

If you're giving the stocking as a gift, fill it with small treasures that would please the recipient: seed packets and a pair of gloves for a gardener; pencils, pens, and notepads for a teacher; penny candy for someone with a sweet tooth.

scented sugars

Granulated sugars infused with the heady taste of vanilla bean, the bright flavor of lemon, or the spicy aroma of cinnamon are quick to make and special to receive. Package the pretty sugars in clear mason jars where they'll keep for months, ready for spooning into coffee or tea, shaken onto cereal or fruit, or sprinkled onto cookies before baking.

For the vanilla sugar, combine 2 cups sugar and 1 1/2 vanilla beans, cut into 2-inch lengths, in a food processor. Process until the vanilla beans are finely chopped. Strain the sugar through a fine-mesh sieve to remove any large pieces of vanilla bean. Let stand for a few days before using so that the sugar becomes infused with the heady aroma of vanilla.

For the lemon sugar, use a vegetable peeler to remove the peel from 1 lemon in wide strips. Set out to dry overnight. Combine the lemon peel with 2 cups sugar in a bowl, then transfer to mason jars or other covered containers. Let stand for a few days before using so the sugar becomes infused with the lemon flavor.

For the cinnamon sugar, divide 2 cups sugar among mason jars or other containers. Insert 1 cinnamon stick into each jar. Let stand for a few days before using so that the sugar becomes infused with the spicy aroma of the cinnamon. Alternatively, combine 2 cups sugar with 2 tablespoons (or more to taste) ground cinnamon and divide among mason jars or other containers.

The scented sugars are beautiful in their simplicity and require little embellishment other than a ribbon and a gift tag. Include suggestions for using the sugar on the gift tag. You can create a scented sugar sampler by assembling the three varieties in a Shaker box and nesting them in colorful tissue. This would make a lovely gift for a baker—or for anybody with a sweet tooth.

christmas potpourri

Did you know that Saint Nicholas was the patron saint of sailors? Greek and Russian seamen, in particular, always sailed with the icon of Saint Nicholas on their ships, and Italian and Dutch sailors purportedly introduced Saint Nicholas to the West. No doubt he was watching over the sailors when they sailed home from other exotic locales with their ships laden with fragrant spices.

Indeed, if Christmas were a scent, it would be a spicy one. This potpourri is redolent with the holiday aromas of orange, cinnamon, and cloves. I like to make a big batch and set it in bowls throughout the house. It's nice to give, too. Pack it in an old-fashioned pottery mixing bowl, or make sachets from muslin and tuck them into a gift box. They will scent clothes drawers, closets—even cars!

MAKES ABOUT 6 CUPS

4 thin-skinned (juicing) oranges

2 lemons

2 cups whole cloves

2 ounces (4 tablespoons) orange
essential oil, or more if desired

1 ounce (2 tablespoons) cinnamon essential oil, or more if desired

10 cinnamon sticks

1 cup whole star anise

1 cup miniature pinecones (available in craft stores)

Using a vegetable peeler, remove the peel from the oranges and lemons in wide strips. Stick the whole cloves in the peels, spacing them about 1 inch apart. Combine the orange and cinnamon essential oils in a small bowl. Dip the orange and lemon peels in the oils, allowing the excess to drip off. Place the citrus peels in a large bowl. Repeat the dipping process with the cinnamon sticks. Add the star anise and the pinecones to the bowl and toss gently to combine. If not using right away, store in a covered container.

To package the potpourri as a gift, spoon it into a small bowl. (During the year, keep your eyes peeled for old pottery bowls such as yellowware or ironstone at tag sales. They hold the potpourri beautifully.) Wrap the bowl in muslin or cellophane and tie with twine or ribbon.

sugar and creamer posies

Flowers that bloom only around Christmastime were considered sacred in countries such as Italy and France. Amid the cold and darkness of the season, a flowering plant signaled that warmth and light were to come.

Amaryllises and paper whites are particularly appealing during the holidays. One lends vibrant color, the other vivid scent. They're easy to force, or coax, to bloom, and your children will enjoy watching their progress until pop! a flower blossoms. The blooms make wonderful natural decorations for your home or someone else's.

Here's an easy way to dress up these popular seasonal flowers for the holidays. Look for sugar bowls and creamers (gravy boats and large teacups work well, too) at flea markets and secondhand stores. Wash each one well. Place one amaryllis bulb or a few paper white bulbs in each vessel (use larger vessels for amaryllis). Fill with small stones or marbles (available at nurseries). Water well. Place in a sunny window and keep damp. In a few weeks, you will be rewarded with beautiful blooms.

Wrap your gift in clear cellophane and finish it with a bow. Include care instructions on the gift tag: "Set this paper white (or amaryllis) in a sunny window and keep damp."

saltwater taffy wreath

Wreaths are not only a Christmas tradition. They signify welcome and unity whenever and wherever they are hung. Candy wreaths, on the other hand, appear to be a distinctly American tradition. References to candy wreaths and the instructions for making them appear in American women's magazines dating back to the early twentieth century. Saltwater taffy is the ideal candy "medium" for such a wreath because it is easy to work with and colorful.

To make the wreath, purchase a Styrofoam wreath form and a supply of saltwater taffy sufficient to cover it. Attach the wrapped candies to the wreath form by inserting one end of a toothpick halfway into the candy and the other into the wreath. Nestle the candies closely together. Fill in the uncovered parts of the form by gluing or pinning crumpled tissue paper onto them. If you wish, add a bow.

You can hang the wreath with picture hangers (available at hardware stores) or simply lay it on a table. When guests come by to visit, invite them to help themselves to the saltwater taffy. Children, especially, like to pluck their favorite colored candy from the wreath and guess its flavor.

This candy wreath would be a thoughtful gift for anybody, but particularly for somebody who hails from the East Coast where saltwater taffy is the pride of the Eastern seaboard—or New Jersey at least.

advent calendar tree

The season of Advent, which means arrival, begins the fourth Sunday before Christmas. A time of anticipation, churches use a wreath decorated with five candles to mark the passing of each week. One candle is lit each of the four weeks, and the fifth candle is lit on Christmas Day.

Advent calendars are based on this same premise, but they have a more secular association. They help young children—and maybe adults, too—count the days until Christmas. This Advent calendar is a three-dimensional tree that serves as a holiday decoration, too.

Make the tree by anchoring bare branches in a sand-filled planter to resemble a tree. The size of the planter will depend on the number and weight of the bare branches, but you will definitely want to fill it almost to the top with sand. If you wish, top the sand with moss (available at nurseries). Choose twenty-five small envelopes in the color of your choice (2$^{1}/_{2}$-by-3-inch envelopes, available at stationery stores, work well for this) and number them from one to twenty-five on the outside front, where you would normally write an address. Fill the envelopes with a handwritten wish (May snow tickle your nose) or instructions for a silly activity (Sing "Jingle Bells" while you hop on one foot) and a candy treat such as a peppermint or a gold foil–wrapped chocolate coin. Hang the envelopes on the branches with binder or easel clips (available in office-supply stores). If you wish, hang small ornaments on the branches, too.

Each day in December, open one envelope (multiple children in a household may, of course, take turns) until Christmas.

This Advent tree is a wonderful gift to give someone just before December. Along with its beauty, it endows a house with a sense of anticipation—and that's a gift that a person of any age will enjoy.

holiday paper lanterns

Strung outdoors across a porch or inside in a doorway, bobbing paper lanterns are a happy way to say "Merry Christmas."

To make the holiday lanterns, purchase white paper Japanese lanterns in the size of your choice at a party-supply store. Working freehand or with a stencil, and using acrylic paint or markers in a dark color, draw a holiday symbol, such as Christmas tree or a reindeer, or write a holiday greeting on each of the lanterns. The bigger and bolder the decoration, the better.

String the lanterns where desired. If you wish, fit them over Christmas lights (the larger bulbs work best) and secure the lanterns with florist's wire. When the lights are illuminated, the decoration appears in silhouette. These paper lanterns would make a merry greeting for guests arriving for the Tree-Trimming Open House (page 100).

yarn surprises

The holiday notions that Victorians gave were not ornate, but they were thoughtful. The act of opening the gift was as important as the gift itself. Sometimes the gift would be affixed to the end of a long piece of yarn that was wrapped every which way around furniture and under tables. The recipient would be given one end of the yarn and instructed to follow the maze to his or her prize at the other end.

In another variation, a small gift was wrapped inside a ball of yarn. The recipient unwound the yarn ball to find his or her surprise inside.

To fashion your own yarn surprises, which can be anything from costume jewelry or a tiny ornament to a foil-wrapped chocolate, hold or tape one end of the yarn on the gift. Wrap the yarn in a circular motion around the gift until a nice, plump ball of yarn forms. If you wish, attach a gift tag.

For multiple gifts, choose various colors of yarn, either a Christmas medley of red, green, and white or a modern palette of hot pink, bright orange, and turquoise. Pile the yarn balls in a big bowl and invite everyone to partake in the fun.

sharing *and* savoring

•

joyful gatherings *that* **celebrate** *the* season

For many of us, Christmas would not be Christmas without a party. The act of coming together to toast the season and share good wishes for the coming year is both reassuring and revitalizing.

The gatherings in this section run the holiday gamut. You can enjoy a fantastical white Christmas Eve dinner that balances the sophisticated with the childlike, or opt for a traditional Christmas Day celebration whose menu harks back to Victorian England. Hosting a party for a crowd? The tree-trimming open house offers a relaxed finger-food buffet for friends and neighbors. The casual fondue menu is just right for a snowy day when all you want to do is sit by the fire with a few close friends.

As December rolls on, you may find yourself a bit peaked. This is the time to summon your girlfriends for a soup-and-sandwiches gift-wrapping party. While they're there, corral them into helping you host a cookie-decorating afternoon for the kids later in the week. Both gatherings will bring you pleasure while supplying two holiday essentials: wrapped gifts and decorated cookies.

As you peruse these gatherings, you'll find that my cooking and decorating style is relaxed, with an eye toward creating delicious food that is served in beautiful ways in festive settings.

Along with the menus, you'll find ideas and instructions for table settings and decorations that create the right mood for each gathering. From party favors and fanciful centerpieces to napkin rings and place cards, you'll see that often it's the smallest elements that deliver the biggest "wow."

Before embarking on any of the menus, one thing you can do that will ensure your sanity is to make a timetable. Working backward, determine when you want to serve the main course and plan from there. For example, for the traditional Christmas Day dinner, if you want the roast beef on the table at 7:00 p.m. and it needs 85 minutes in the oven, plus an additional 15 minutes resting time while the Yorkshire pudding bakes, you know that you must put the beef in the preheated oven (don't forget to plan 10 minutes for preheating!) at 5:20 p.m. The sweet potato fingers can roast with the beef during its last 25 minutes of cooking. You can prepare the creamed spinach on the stove top while the Yorkshire pudding bakes in the oven. Because it can "hold" and still maintain its flavor and shape, the dessert, a *bûche de Noël,* can be made the day before and frozen. Make the shrimp cocktail appetizer earlier in the day, and the hors d'oeuvres and the horseradish sauce at around 4:00 p.m. This will give you time for a shower plus, if you're lucky, a few quiet moments to yourself before the guests arrive.

Here's another simple, stress-reducing, time-saving trick. Did you ever notice how much time you spend in the market during the holidays? Did you also notice that it is probably the most crowded time of the year to be there? Pare minutes and stress off the visit by compiling a list that mimics the floor plan of the store. Make categories based on the departments, such as produce and paper goods. Read through your recipes and jot down your needs under the appropriate categories. When you visit the market, wheel your cart from one side of the store to the other, visiting each of the departments as you work through your list. You will leave the market less harried, I guarantee it.

Taking a few minutes to plan will increase your enjoyment whether you're cooking or decorating or making gifts. As my dad always told me, "Timing is everything." Yes, and so is time. Spend more of it with the people you love.

White Christmas Eve Dinner

This dinner is not inspired by a single tradition, but rather by the mythical appeal of a snowy Christmas Eve. Whether it's the snow (real or imagined) or the keen sense of anticipation that imbues everything with a magical quality, I can't say. I just know that, like a child, I look forward to this extraordinary night all year long.

Nothing compares to Christmas Eve. Guests arrive dressed up and jovial, and children emerge from their baths red-cheeked and glowing with excitement. For me, it's the best gift of the season.

The scene for this dinner mimics the children's sense of Christmas magic and their belief that anything can happen at anytime. First, I cover the table with white faux fur fabric. I sprinkle faux snow on it (talk about gilding the lily!). The scene is punctuated with tiny bottle brush evergreen trees. Clear glass hurricane candleholders are filled with kosher salt to resemble snow, and pillar candles are nestled in them. You can tip the hurricane holders to create snowdrifts.

Where there is snow, there are snowmen. Just so things don't get too sophisticated and stodgy (this is Christmas Eve with all its childhood connotations after all), I jolt the table with a bevy of snowmen and brilliant pink color. A jolly carnation snowman (page 62), complete with pink polka dot ribbon scarf, is set on the table as a centerpiece and focal point. He perches happily in a pedestal container so he can survey the festivities around him. (Figures of snowmen, some vintage, some not, gambol around his "snowy" kingdom.) The kids adore it.

Each place setting includes a snowman-shaped napkin ring made by the children from pink and white pipe cleaners and copper cookie cutters (page 58). For mementos of this enchanting night, there are matchboxes decorated with silver glitter and pom-pom snowmen and filled with small pink and white candies along with a Christmas wish (page 60).

Little white lights in the shape of snowflakes are everywhere! They border the doors to the dining room and adorn the French doors to the porch. They are strung along the ceiling molding, too. The glittery white of the room is complemented by the shimmering sound of silver bells threaded on pink satin ribbon and hung from the back of each chair.

Once everybody has arrived, I serve my Christmas version of pink champagne cocktails (page 48) along with pistachios and warm cheese toasts (page 50). The cheese toasts remind me of my late—and hilariously funny—Irish grandmother who could take something as simple as this recipe and turn it into an occasion—the mark of an excellent hostess. The pairing of champagne and cheese toasts is the signal that the evening will be a little bit "dress up" and a lot of fun!

The first course is a Christmas soup (page 52). I call it Christmas soup for the sole reason that it is green with a sprinkling of diced red pepper and grated Parmesan cheese "snow" on top. Broccoli and leeks compose this creamy, fresh-tasting soup that gets most of its richness from potatoes rather than cream. It's a festive way to begin dinner.

My dad is Italian and, because Italians traditionally eat seafood on Christmas Eve, we did too. Today, the evening just wouldn't be the same without it, and shellfish gratins (page 54) are a particularly delicious way to celebrate the custom. Serving food in gratin dishes automatically elevates the occasion to a special one. Fill them with a rich and creamy shellfish mixture topped with buttery bread crumbs and you know it's a no-holds-barred holiday dinner! The gratins are accompanied with a refreshingly simple butter lettuce salad dressed with champagne vinaigrette (page 55).

Dessert is a whimsical vanilla-coconut snowman cake (page 57). It's delicious and ends the evening on an appropriately child-friendly note. With the coffee, I pass bowls of silver-wrapped Hershey Kisses and plates of fluffy marshmallows just for fun.

christmas champagne cocktail

Bubbles and the holidays are a match made in heaven. Hence, this bubbly beverage to commence the festivities. If you want a rosier cocktail, pour pink champagne. For the children, substitute sparkling cider for the champagne.

SERVES 1

1 lemon wedge
¼ cup pink decorating sugar
1 sugar cube
dash of pomegranate nectar
chilled champagne, or other sparkling wine or sparkling cider

Rub the rim of a champagne flute with the lemon wedge, then dip the rim into the decorating sugar (save any extra sugar for making more cocktails). Put the sugar cube into the flute. Drop the pomegranate nectar on the sugar. Pour in the sparkling wine or cider to fill the glass. Serve immediately.

santa's coming

Before your guests arrive and when your children are in the bath (with an adult watching them, of course!), steal outside and hide a string of jingle bells under their bedroom windows. When your children are in their beds and have settled down a bit from the evening's festivities, sneak outside and shake the bells. They'll be beside themselves with excitement!

warm cheese toasts

If you dropped into an Irish household in the late nineteenth century, whether it was Christmastime or not, chances are you would have been offered a cheese toast on homemade brown bread. Old-fashioned yet somehow still appropriate, cheese toasts are timeless in their appeal—and just right for this Christmas Eve celebration. Set out bowls of pistachios for enjoying along with the toasts.

SERVES 6

1 sweet baguette, cut into 1/4-inch-thick slices
1/2 cup extra-virgin olive oil
1/2 cup freshly grated Parmesan cheese
1/2 cup grated Gruyère cheese
1/2 cup crumbled blue cheese such as Roquefort

Preheat the oven to 400°F.

Brush the bread slices on one side with the olive oil and place in a single layer on a baking sheet. Bake, turning once, until just beginning to become golden, about 2 minutes on each side. Remove from the oven and sprinkle with the cheeses, topping an equal number of bread slices with each kind of cheese. Return to the oven and continue to bake just until the cheese melts, 3 to 5 minutes.

To serve, line a platter with a cloth napkin and arrange the cheese toasts on it. Serve immediately.

christmas soup

It's a paradox I know, but this soup actually manages to be rich and creamy and good for you at the same time. Broccoli, leeks, and parsley lend both flavor and color, and potatoes give it luscious texture. Use star-shaped cookie cutters to make star croutons for floating on top.

SERVES 6

3/4 cup (1 1/2 sticks) unsalted butter

2 tablespoons olive oil

3 leeks, well rinsed and coarsely chopped

1 large yellow onion, chopped

3 cloves garlic, minced

8 cups chicken stock or canned chicken broth

2 red potatoes, peeled and diced

2 large bunches broccoli (about 3 pounds total weight), trimmed and stems and florets coarsely chopped

1 1/4 cups freshly grated Parmesan cheese

1/2 cup chopped fresh flat-leaf parsley

1/8 teaspoon red pepper flakes

salt and freshly ground pepper

1/2 to 3/4 cup heavy cream

1 large red bell pepper, finely diced

In a large pot over low heat, melt the butter with the olive oil. Add the leeks, onion, and garlic and cook, stirring occasionally, until the vegetables are very soft, about 15 minutes.

Add the stock and potatoes, increase the heat to medium, and cook, uncovered, until the potatoes are tender, about 15 minutes. Add the broccoli and cook until tender, about 10 minutes. Remove from the heat and stir in 1 cup of the Parmesan, the parsley, the red pepper flakes, and the salt and ground pepper to taste. Let stand for 3 minutes.

Working in batches, puree the soup in a food processor or a blender. Return the soup to the pan and whisk in the cream in a slow, steady stream. Rewarm the soup over low heat.

To serve, ladle the soup into serving bowls. Garnish evenly with the diced red pepper and the remaining 1/4 cup Parmesan cheese.

shellfish gratins

Feel free to vary the shellfish selection, or use only one type if you wish. If you don't have individual dishes, don't fret. Simply spoon the cooked mixture into a 1½-quart oval gratin baking dish and proceed as directed, increasing the total baking time to about 15 minutes, or until heated through. None of the magic will be lost—promise.

SERVES 6

4 tablespoons (½ stick) unsalted butter, plus
    ¾ cup (1½ sticks), cut into small pieces
1 small yellow onion, finely chopped
1½ cups finely chopped mushrooms
¼ cup all-purpose flour
1½ cups half-and-half
½ cup dry sherry
2 teaspoons dry mustard
4 egg yolks

salt and freshly ground pepper
½ pound crabmeat, picked over well to remove
    any bits of shell
½ pound small shrimp, peeled and deveined
½ pound lobster meat, picked over to remove
    any bits of shell
1½ cups fresh bread crumbs
Lemon wedges

Preheat the oven to 400°F.

In a saucepan over medium heat, melt 4 tablespoons of the butter. When it begins to foam, add the onion and the mushrooms and cook until the onion is translucent, about 5 minutes. Add the flour and cook, stirring, for 3 minutes. Add the half-and-half, sherry, and dry mustard and cook, stirring constantly, until the mixture thickens and is smooth, about 8 minutes.

Put the yolks in a small bowl and stir about ¼ cup of the sauce into them. Add the salt and pepper to taste to this mixture and pour back into the pan, mixing thoroughly. Do not let the mixture boil (reduce the heat if necessary).

Add all the shellfish and heat until warmed through. Divide the mixture evenly among six ¾-cup gratin dishes or ramekins. Top with the bread crumbs and dot with the ¾ cup butter. Bake the gratins until the shellfish is hot and the crumbs are brown, 5 to 10 minutes. Serve immediately accompanied with lemon wedges.

butter lettuce salad with champagne vinaigrette

A luxurious main course calls for an equally elegant salad. It's nothing more than simple greens adorned with a lively champagne vinaigrette, but it fits the bill perfectly. Choose the delicate— and aptly named—butter lettuce for this salad. It makes a difference.

SERVES 6

Champagne Vinaigrette

2 tablespoons champagne vinegar

6 tablespoons extra-virgin olive oil

1 tablespoon finely chopped shallot

1 tablespoon finely chopped fresh tarragon, or $1/2$ teaspoon crumbled dried tarragon

salt and freshly ground pepper

8 cups butter (Bibb) lettuce, torn into bite-size pieces

2 Belgian endives, rimmed and cut into bite-size pieces

1 bunch watercress, trimmed

To make the vinaigrette, in a small bowl, whisk together the vinegar and olive oil. Stir in the shallot, tarragon, and the salt and pepper to taste.

Pour the vinaigrette into the bottom of a salad bowl. Add the lettuce, endive, and watercress and toss to coat with the dressing. Serve immediately.

snowman cake

This is a variation of the classic 1-2-3-4 cake that traditionally includes 1 cup butter, 2 cups sugar, 3 cups flour, and 4 eggs. It's moist and tender and just plain delicious. Drifts of shredded coconut and candy features adorn this frosty gent. Be sure to decorate the cake on the platter on which you will serve it, as it will be too difficult to move it once you have finished. Children will get a kick out of decorating the snowman.

SERVES 6, WITH LEFTOVERS

3 cups sifted cake flour (not self-rising)

1 tablespoon baking powder

1/2 teaspoon salt

1 cup (2 sticks) unsalted butter, softened

2 cups sugar

4 eggs

1 1/2 teaspoons pure almond extract

1 cup whole milk

Seven-Minute Icing

2 egg whites

1 1/4 cups superfine sugar

1/4 teaspoon cream of tartar

pinch of salt

1 tablespoon pure vanilla extract

1 1/2 cups sweetened shredded coconut

2 small chocolate peppermint patties

red licorice twist such as Twizzler

1 large orange gumdrop

3 round peppermint candies

fruit leather

2 small branches

Preheat the oven to 350°F. Butter and flour two 9-inch round cake pans. Tap out the excess flour.

In a bowl, whisk together the cake flour, baking powder, and salt; reserve.

In a large bowl, using an electric mixer set on medium-high speed, beat together the butter and the sugar until light and fluffy. Beat in the eggs one at a time. Beat in the almond extract. Reduce the mixer speed to low and beat in the flour mixture in three batches, alternating with the milk.

continued

Divide the batter evenly between the two prepared pans, smoothing the tops with a rubber spatula. Bake until the center of each cake springs back when touched gently and the edges are golden brown and pulling away from the sides of the pan, 25 to 30 minutes.

Remove the cakes from the oven and let cool completely in the pans on wire racks. Run a knife around the inside edges of the pans to loosen the cakes, then turn the cakes out onto a flat platter large enough for the two rounds to sit side by side, or onto a large piece of cardboard covered with aluminum foil or decorative wrap.

To make the snowman, draw a 7-inch circle on one piece of cardboard and an 8-inch circle on another piece of cardboard. Place the 7-inch cardboard circle on one of the cake layers and cut around it (this is the head). Place the 8-inch cardboard circle on the remaining cake layer and cut around it (this is the body). Discard (or eat) the excess cake.

To make the icing, place the egg whites, sugar, cream of tartar, and salt in the top of a double boiler set over gently simmering water. Using an electric mixer set on medium speed, beat until the frosting forms stiff peaks, 3 to 4 minutes. Remove from the heat and stir in the vanilla extract. Continue to beat until the icing is glossy and thick enough to spread, about 2 minutes longer. You should have about 2 cups. Frost the tops and sides of both cake layers with it. Before the icing hardens, pat the coconut into the frosting, then push the cakes together so they look like the head and body of a snowman. On the smaller cake, make the eyes with the two peppermint patties, the mouth with the red licorice, and the nose with the gumdrop. On the larger cake, make the buttons with the peppermint candies. Cut out a bow tie from the fruit leather and put it in place. Finally, insert the branches into the snowman for his arms.

pink snowman napkin rings

To make each napkin ring, wrap 2 pipe cleaners (pink and/or white) around the outside of a 4-inch cookie cutter, fitting them snugly to form the snowman shape. Twist the pipe cleaners at the bottom of the snowman to secure, then clip the ends. Fit the napkin into the napkin ring.

matchbox favors

* 1 small matchbox
* paintbrush
* white acrylic paint
* silver glitter
* craft glue
* 3 white pom-poms or cotton balls, each 1/2 inch in diameter
* scissors
* construction paper in assorted colors
* small pink and white candies

Remove the inner portion of the matchbox; reserve. Using the paintbrush and the white acrylic paint, paint the exterior of the outer matchbox. Let dry almost completely, then sprinkle silver glitter over all the painted surfaces. Let stand for 5 minutes, then shake off the excess glitter.

Using the craft glue, attach the white pom-poms or cotton balls onto the top of the matchbox to form a snowman. Using the scissors and the construction paper, cut out eyes, nose, mouth, buttons, and hat, and glue them to the snowman with the craft glue. Fill the reserved inner matchbox with small candies, slip in a Christmas wish written on a small piece of paper, and then slide the interior portion of the box into the glittery cover.

carnation snowman

This jolly snowman has two faces, so he pleases both sides of the table. If you wish, you can make only one face. This centerpiece can be made a day ahead of time and refrigerated.

FOR THE SNOWMAN, YOU WILL NEED:

* 2 rounds floral foam, one about 12 inches in diameter to sit snugly in the container that will hold the body and the other slightly smaller for the snowman's head
* pedestal container, about 12 inches in diameter
* 8 to 12 floral sticks, each 18 inches long
* toothpicks
* about 6 dozen white carnations, depending on bloom size
* 10 malted milk balls
* 2 small carrots (or the tips of larger carrots)
* 12 whole cranberries
* 1 yard pink wired (French) ribbon

Soak both rounds of floral foam in water according to package directions. Place the larger foam round in the container. Secure the smaller foam round to the larger round with the floral sticks, breaking the sticks if they are too long.

Working from the bottom up, insert the carnations into the foam at an angle. The stems should be 4 to 5 inches long on the bottom and 3 to 4 inches long on the top.

On the front of the snowman, use toothpicks to attach his eyes, nose, and mouth: Insert one end of a toothpick into a malted milk ball and the other end into the snowman for an eye. Repeat with another malted milk ball for the second eye. Use this same process with the carrot for the nose, the cranberries for the mouth, and more malted milk balls for the buttons. Add a face and buttons to the opposite side of the snowman, too.

Cut the ribbon in half. Use each half to tie a scarf around the snowman's neck, tying one on each side.

Old-Fashioned Christmas Breakfast

You were roused by the kids at 5 A.M. after staying up past midnight to assemble "Santa's gifts," and you've lived through the happy frenzy of opening presents. Now, everybody is ready for a hearty breakfast.

When more of our nation's people were rural rather than urban, work did not stop on Christmas Day. Breakfast was the opportunity for farm families to greet the holiday in a special way before they went about their chores. It's nice to remember this tie to the rural world and to think about those people who, on this Christmas Day, are working on our behalf.

An old-fashioned farmhouse breakfast offers a deliciously relaxed way to begin this joyful day. Usually, it's just our immediate family at home on Christmas morning, and making breakfast together is a fun way for us to begin our Christmas Day celebration.

The menu is both robust and nostalgic. When my sisters and I were kids, our dad always made silver dollar pancakes (page 68) for us. We loved it! Your kids will love them, too. Of course you can use a packaged pancake mix, but, really, the batter is so

easy to make from scratch and it tastes better, too, so the little extra effort is worth it. I also offer you a quick way to make a spice butter that will give the pancakes a holiday twist.

But the doughnut holes (page 75)! Until you have had a warm, sugary doughnut hole, you have not lived. Making these little bites of heaven can easily turn into a holiday tradition for you and your family. It's best if the kids punch out the holes and the adults fry them. Everybody can shake the warm doughnut holes in the sugar and pop them into their mouths.

Add sugar bacon (page 71) and freshly squeezed tangerine juice to the menu and you have got a complete breakfast. Unless of course you want more—and who wouldn't? I have also included a recipe for Egg Strata with Goat Cheese and Herbs (page 73), a make-ahead dish that marries eggs, cheese, herbs, and bread in a bread puddinglike casserole.

We enjoy this casual breakfast in the kitchen or in front of the fireplace in the family room. The simply decorated table reflects two traditions we celebrate each year. The first, in keeping with the farmhouse theme, showcases animals. Did you know that long ago some cultures believed that the animals could speak on Christmas Day? I have tested this on our two Labrador retrievers, Saba and Feather, but so far, silence. Instead, during December we make animal place mats (page 77) and set our breakfast table with them. I collect the place mats after breakfast and save them to give to my son when he has his own children. You can also give them to a grandparent or other relative who will undoubtedly appreciate the artistic potential they reflect.

In France and other European countries, Santa does not slide down the chimney. Perhaps he accumulates too much weight as he eats his way through all the treats that the children leave for him on his all-night journey. Instead, children put their shoes outside the front door and Santa stuffs small gifts into them (and slips the rest of the gifts under the tree). In our house, I bring this tradition to life with new slippers for each family member. Before we sit down to breakfast, I place a pair on each chair and fill them with Christmas candies.

silver dollar buttermilk pancakes with christmas spice butter

The secret to a tender, fluffy pancake lies in not overmixing the batter. The flavored butter, redolent with cinnamon, nutmeg, and allspice, is a nice seasonal touch.

MAKES FORTY-EIGHT 3-INCH PANCAKES; SERVES 6 GENEROUSLY

2 cups all-purpose flour

1 teaspoon baking soda

1 teaspoon salt, plus a pinch more

2 eggs, separated

2 cups buttermilk

4 tablespoons (1/2 stick) unsalted butter, melted and cooled

1/2 teaspoon pure vanilla extract

nonstick cooking spray or vegetable oil for frying

Christmas Spice Butter (page 70)

maple syrup, heated

In a small bowl, stir together the flour, baking soda, and 1 teaspoon salt; reserve.

In a bowl, using an electric mixer set on medium speed, beat the egg yolks with the buttermilk until blended. Add the flour mixture, melted butter, and vanilla extract and beat just until the mixture is smooth; do not overbeat. Reserve.

Rinse and dry the mixer beaters. In a small bowl, combine the egg whites and the pinch of salt. Using the electric mixer set on medium speed, beat the egg whites until soft peaks form. Using a rubber spatula, fold the egg whites into the batter.

Heat a griddle or a large frying pan over medium-high heat and lightly grease it with nonstick cooking spray or vegetable oil. Using a tablespoon, spoon the batter onto the hot griddle, forming as many pancakes as you can without crowding. Each pancake should be about 3 inches in diameter.

Cook the pancakes until the tops are covered with tiny bubbles, the bottoms are browned, and the edges look dry, about 1 minute. Flip them and continue cooking until the second side is golden brown, 30 to 60 seconds more. Transfer to a heatproof platter and keep warm in a 200°F oven until all are cooked.

Serve the pancakes hot with the spice butter and the warm maple syrup.

continued

christmas spice butter

You can vary the spices in this butter according to your own preference. This aromatic butter is delicious on muffins and toast, too. It can be made up to a week ahead of time and covered and refrigerated until ready to use. Bring it to room temperature before serving.

MAKES 1 CUP

1 cup (2 sticks) unsalted butter, softened

1/2 teaspoon ground cinnamon

1/2 teaspoon ground ginger

1/2 teaspoon freshly grated nutmeg

1/4 teaspoon ground allspice

1 tablespoon sugar

In a small bowl, combine all of the ingredients and mix well with a spoon.

sugar bacon

The combination of sweet and salty is a classic culinary pairing. How nice to enjoy this marriage of flavors in your Christmas morning bacon. Make sure you use the best-quality bacon you can find for the tastiest result. It really does make a difference. Kids will love this—guaranteed!

SERVES 6

18 thick slices (about 1 pound) best-quality bacon
$1/2$ cup firmly packed golden brown sugar
2 tablespoons mild mustard

In a large skillet or griddle over medium heat, fry the bacon, turning once, until it just begins to become crispy. Transfer to paper towels to drain.

In a small bowl, stir together the brown sugar and the mustard.

Return the bacon to the skillet or griddle and reduce the heat to low. Brush the sugar mixture over the bacon and continue to cook, turning once, until the bacon is well browned and firm.

Serve immediately. Do not cover the bacon to keep it warm, or it will become sticky and gooey.

egg strata with goat cheese and herbs

This dish is aptly named **strata**, *which means layered, because that's what all the wonderfully savory ingredients do. You can prepare it the night before and refrigerate it until ready to bake.*

SERVES 6

1-pound loaf country bread, crusts removed

2 cups crumbled fresh goat cheese
(about 1/2 pound)

1/2 cup freshly grated Parmesan cheese

1 tablespoon chopped fresh thyme

2 tablespoons chopped fresh flat-leaf parsley

1 tablespoon chopped fresh chives or green tops
of scallions

5 eggs

1 cup half-and-half

few dashes Tabasco or other hot-pepper sauce

3/4 teaspoon salt

1/2 teaspoon freshly ground pepper

4 tablespoons (1/2 stick) unsalted butter,
melted and cooled

Butter a 9-inch round or square baking dish.

Cut the bread into 1/2-inch-thick slices; reserve. In a small bowl, mix together the goat cheese and the Parmesan cheese; reserve. In another small bowl, stir together the herbs; reserve.

Arrange a layer of bread slices in the bottom of the prepared dish. Top with a layer of cheese and then a layer of herbs. Repeat the layering once or twice more until you have two or three equal layers in all.

In a bowl, whisk together the eggs, half-and-half, Tabasco, salt, and pepper. Pour evenly over the bread mixture. Drizzle with the 4 tablespoons melted butter.
Cover and refrigerate for at least 1 hour or for up to overnight. Remove from the refrigerator 30 minutes before baking.

Preheat the oven to 350°F. Bake the *strata* until it is puffed and golden brown and lightly set in the center, about 50 minutes. Remove from the oven and let sit for 5 minutes before serving.

doughnut holes

To save time on Christmas morning, make the batter the night before and refrigerate it until ready to use. In fact, for the lightest doughnuts, make sure the doughnut holes are cold before frying them.

MAKES 2 DOZEN DOUGHNUT HOLES

2 cups all-purpose flour, plus extra as needed

1 teaspoon freshly grated nutmeg

1 teaspoon baking powder

1/4 teaspoon baking soda

pinch of salt

1 egg

1/2 cup granulated sugar

1/2 cup buttermilk

1 tablespoon unsalted butter, melted and cooled slightly

1/2 teaspoon pure vanilla extract

vegetable oil such as peanut or canola for deep-frying

2 cups confectioners' sugar

1/4 cup ground cinnamon

Place the 2 cups flour in a large bowl and fluff it with a whisk to aerate it. Add the nutmeg, baking powder, baking soda, and salt and whisk the mixture again to mix well.

In a bowl, using an electric mixer set on medium speed, beat the egg until frothy. With the mixer running, gradually add the granulated sugar, beating until light and fluffy. Add the buttermilk, melted butter, and vanilla extract and mix well.

Make a well in the center of the flour mixture. Pour the egg mixture into the well and mix thoroughly with your hands or a wooden spoon. The dough should be soft but not sticky. Continue to add small amounts of flour until the dough reaches the desired consistency.

Lightly flour a work surface. Transfer the dough to the work surface and dust the top of it very lightly with flour. Roll out the dough about 1/3 inch thick. Dip the removable center of a doughnut cutter or a 1 1/2-inch round biscuit or cookie cutter into flour and then cut out the doughnut holes. As you do so, transfer the holes with a spatula to a baking sheet or platter. Reroll the scraps to cut out more doughnut holes. Cover with plastic wrap and refrigerate for at least 3 hours or up to overnight.

continued

Pour the oil to a depth of 3 inches into a deep-fat fryer or a heavy, deep saucepan and heat to 375°F on a deep-frying thermometer. (Alternatively, carefully drop a doughnut hole into the oil and fry until golden brown, 1½ to 2 minutes. Drain the doughnut hole briefly on paper towels and break it open. If it's not cooked through, the oil is too hot. If it's very greasy, the oil is not hot enough.)

Working in small batches (do not crowd the doughnut holes!), carefully place the doughnut holes in the hot oil and fry, turning them gently with tongs, until golden brown, 1½ to 2 minutes. Using a slotted spoon, transfer to paper towels to drain until cool enough to handle.

Place 1 cup of the confectioners' sugar in a small paper bag. Place the remaining 1 cup confectioners' sugar and the cinnamon in another small paper bag and shake gently to mix. Just before serving, shake half of the warm doughnut holes in the bag with the plain sugar and the other half with the cinnamon sugar.

Arrange the doughnut holes on a cake stand or platter. Serve warm.

animal place mats

These simple-to-make place mats evoke the magical notion that animals can speak on Christmas Day. Even if that's just a fantasy, these colorful mats will decorate your breakfast table or make a sweet gift for an animal lover. This is a great family activity.

FOR EACH PLACE MAT, YOU WILL NEED:

* pencil
* ruler
* 1 piece red felt, about 16 inches square, for mat
* scissors
* cookie cutters or stencils in animal shapes
* felt pieces, in additional colors, for animals
* fabric markers
* glitter (optional)
* beads (optional)
* buttons (optional)
* craft glue

Using the pencil and ruler, draw a simple barn shape on the large piece of felt. Cut it out with the scissors. Using cookie cutters or stencils, trace animal shapes on the additional pieces of felt and cut them out. Decorate the animals with the fabric markers and the glitter, beads, and buttons, if using, attaching them with craft glue to the barn mat.

If you're using the mats for your family's breakfast, write each family member's name on his or her mat with fabric marker. If you're giving the place mats as a gift, write a holiday greeting on the mats with a fabric marker. Include the date, too, if you wish.

Extravagant feasts have played a key role in celebrations since the winter solstice festivals long ago. In medieval England, the standard celebratory winter feast centered on roasted oxen (served whole!), boar's head, and all manner of wild animals. But the Christmas dinner menu that most of us categorize as "classic" comes to us from the Victorian English. Once a year, the table would be laid with foods that were as spectacular in presentation as they were in taste, including turkey, goose, and the roast beef and Yorkshire pudding that are part of this menu. The table was decorated in equal fashion. The house looked festive and so did the guests.

It is with this same spirit that I like to have a traditional Christmas dinner in the late afternoon of Christmas Day. The gifts have been opened, the naps have been taken, and a hush descends on the house.

But this is by no means a sedate dinner. It's simply one filled with the nourishing satisfaction of communing with the familiar in all its manifestations, from young children gleefully playing "camp" under the table to elder guests toasting old memories. There is certain comfort born from years of expecting and enjoying the same foods and, often, the same company.

I like to serve this Christmas dinner just after the sun has set. There is a fire in the fireplace and lighted candles are everywhere. The glow is both warm and magical, and it makes everybody feel embraced by the special spirit of Christmas night.

This is a traditional English menu with two exceptions, one to begin the dinner and one to end it: shrimp cocktail (page 84), a decidedly American appetizer, and *bûche de Noël* (page 92), a distinctly French dessert. It's a bit of gustatory license as well as a nod to our nation's "melting pot" heritage. All of the recipes in this menu, with the exception of the *bûche de Noël*, may be doubled, if you are entertaining a crowd.

Shrimp cocktail manages to be both sophisticated and fun, and it seems that everybody—adults and children—likes shrimp. It's a great way to commence a holiday dinner that shares the same characteristics.

The spectacular centerpiece for this holiday dinner is roast prime rib of beef (page 85). It's accompanied by golden Yorkshire pudding puffs (page 88), sumptuous creamed spinach (page 90), and roasted sweet potato fingers (page 91). A horseradish cream whip (page 87) is a nice counterpoint to the richness of the roast.

Dessert is a *bûche de Noël*, the traditional chocolate Yule log, or cake, here filled with peppermint stick ice cream, iced with glossy chocolate frosting, and decorated with marzipan mushrooms and sugared cranberries. At once fantastical and lavish, it is a confectionery replica of the once-popular Yule log tradition. On Christmas Eve, families would scour the woods to find a large log that they would burn in their fireplaces through the twelve days of Christmas to ensure good fortune in the coming year. Each year, the log was lit with a piece of burned Yule log saved from the previous year (this guaranteed the continuity of good fortune).

By the time dinner ends, the children have returned to their toys. For those adults who wish to linger, I serve Stilton cheese and glasses of port and Madeira.

After this long day, nobody feels like being constricted by formality, so I set a table that is both cheerful and comforting. The focal point is the family Christmas china that comes out only once a year. When I unwrap the china, I feel as if I am greeting an old friend. I mix it with well-worn hotel silver picked up over the years at flea markets and old crystal wineglasses. Candles are anchored in candlesticks that match the Christmas china. I set bobeches made from cranberries (page 97) on the candlesticks to catch the melting wax. The table glows.

Petite Christmas trees mark the place settings. Fashioned from evergreen boughs that we clipped on an afternoon walk a few days before, they're a snap to make. Press damp floral foam into a waterproof container (we used tiny clay flowerpots), then insert the boughs and arrange them to look like a Christmas tree.

For the place cards, I adopted a Victorian custom. The Victorians created ornate place cards for their guests. These place cards were made from fancy paper, seals, and sealing wax. At the end of the meal, they invited their guests to hang them on the Christmas tree.

Using sealing wax and initialed seals (available in stationery stores), drip wax onto plain white place cards and stamp each guest's first initial onto his or her place card (give the stamp as a party favor). Or opt to use your family's initial only.

After dinner, ask each guest to write a wish on his or her place card before putting it on the tree. When you dismantle your tree, collect the cards and save them until next year when the guests can check if their wishes came true.

Of course, Christmas crackers (page 98) are a must. Here's how to perform the Christmas cracker ritual: Instruct your guests to cross their arms and hold one end of their Christmas cracker in one hand. The guest sitting to the person's right holds the other end. Everybody makes a wish and, on the count of three, pulls the cracker ends. Let the festivities begin!

egg and caviar canapés

Did you know that in French canapé means "sofa"? How perfect! The toast round, the base of any canapé, is the sofa for the food it carries into your mouth. Délicieux! If you want to make these nibbles extra Christmasy, cut the bread into Christmas tree shapes with a cookie cutter before assembling the canapés, then garnish the finished canapé trees with red salmon roe to resemble tiny ornaments. This recipe can be doubled easily.

MAKES 12 CANAPÉS; SERVES 6

4 slices firmly textured white bread
2 tablespoons unsalted butter, melted and cooled
yolks from 4 hard-boiled eggs
2 tablespoons grated yellow onion
1 teaspoon dry mustard
about 2 tablespoons crème frâiche or sour cream
salt and freshly ground pepper
2 ounces caviar or salmon roe

Preheat the oven to 400°F.

Using a 2-inch round cookie cutter, cut out twelve rounds from the bread. Lightly brush one side with the melted butter. Transfer to baking sheets and bake until golden brown, 8 to 10 minutes. Remove from the oven and transfer to cooling racks.

In a bowl, using a spoon, mash the egg yolks with the onion and dry mustard. Stir in just enough crème frâiche or sour cream to bind the mixture. Season to taste with salt and pepper.

Spread the egg yolk mixture on the buttered sides of the toast rounds, dividing it evenly. Garnish with the caviar or salmon roe. These are best served within an hour after making.

shrimp cocktail

Whenever I serve shrimp cocktail, I am rewarded with "oohs" and "ahs" from my guests. It's a bit disconcerting since the appetizer is incredibly easy to make—but who's complaining? When it happens to you, just flash a smile and enjoy the kudos. Freshly cooked shrimp will give you better flavor and texture, but if time—or the lack thereof—is a factor, by all means buy precooked, peeled shrimp This recipe may be doubled.

SERVES 6

Sauce

2 cups tomato ketchup

2 tablespoons Worcestershire sauce

3 tablespoons prepared horseradish

2 tablespoons finely minced shallot

$^1/_2$ teaspoon Tabasco or other hot-pepper sauce, or more to taste

salt and freshly ground pepper

fresh lemon juice

36 large shrimp

lemon wedges

buttered toast triangles (optional)

To make the sauce in a bowl, combine the ketchup, Worcestershire sauce, horseradish, shallot, Tabasco, and salt, pepper, and lemon juice to taste. Cover and refrigerate until ready to use.

Place the shrimp in a large, wide, shallow pan, such as a sauté pan, and cover with water. Bring to a boil, reduce the heat to low, and cook just until the shrimp turn pink, about 3 minutes. Do not overcook or the shrimp will be mushy. Drain the shrimp and rinse well under cold water. Peel and devein the shrimp, leaving the tail shell segments intact.

To serve, arrange six shrimp on each plate and garnish with the lemon wedges. Divide the sauce among six small bowls and place a bowl alongside each plate. Pass the toast triangles, if you wish.

roast prime rib of beef
with horseradish cream whip

Many people believe that cooking a roast is difficult. It isn't. The size may be large and therefore intimidating, but a roast is one of the easiest things to cook. All you do is season it and put it in the oven. And if you have an instant-read thermometer, you're golden! It's the surefire way to ensure a perfectly cooked roast.

SERVES 6 TO 8

4-rib standing rib roast, about 6 pounds
1 lemon
salt and freshly ground pepper
1 cup dry red wine
1 tablespoon chopped fresh thyme

Remove the meat from the refrigerator 2 hours before you plan to begin cooking it. Bringing it to room temperature ensures more even cooking.

Preheat the oven to 450°F. Place the meat, bone-side down, in a roasting pan. Cut the lemon in half and rub the cut side of each half all over the beef. Season the roast with salt and pepper.

Roast the meat for 15 minutes. Reduce the heat to 350°F and continue to roast for 70 minutes more. To test for doneness, insert an instant-read thermometer into the thickest part of the roast away from the bone; it should register 125°F. The meat will be rare in the center and medium-rare to medium near the ends. (Note: If you are cooking a roast that is larger than 4 pounds, adjust the cooking time accordingly.)

Remove the meat from the oven, transfer it to a cutting board or platter, and tent it loosely with aluminum foil. Let rest for at least 15 minutes or for up to 45 minutes before carving. (Increase the oven temperature to 450°F to bake the Yorkshire Pudding Puffs, page 88, while the roast rests.)

continued

While the meat is resting, make the sauce: pour off all but a few tablespoons of fat from the roasting pan. Reserve the fat you have poured off for making the Yorkshire pudding puffs. Place the roasting pan on the stove top over high heat. Add the wine and cook, stirring up any browned bits on the bottom of the pan, until the liquid reduces by half. Reduce the heat to low, stir in the thyme, and let the sauce sit for a minute. Pour into a warmed gravy boat or sauce pitcher.

To serve, slice the roast: cut the first slice close to the bone, between the ribs. The second slice will be boneless. Pass the sauce at the table.

horseradish cream whip

Horseradish is a classic accompaniment to roast beef. In this recipe, I combine horseradish with whipped cream to complement the horseradish's flavor and texture and tone down its piquancy for the children. It looks pretty on the table, too. Look for prepared horseradish in your market's refrigerated section; it will be fresher than the one you'll find in the condiment aisle.

MAKES ABOUT 2 CUPS

1^1/$_2$ cups heavy cream
^{1}/$_3$ cup prepared horseradish, plus more to taste
1 teaspoon finely grated lemon zest
freshly ground white pepper

In a bowl, using a whisk or an electric mixer set on medium speed, whip the cream until soft peaks form. Stir in the horseradish, lemon zest, and white pepper to taste. Spoon into a bowl and pass at the table.

yorkshire pudding puffs

The traditional accompaniment to roast prime rib of beef, and definitely a festive addition to the Christmas table, Yorkshire pudding is rich and luscious. Kids go crazy for it! I like to make it in a muffin pan so everybody has his or her own little pudding. You can make the batter up to a day in advance and refrigerate it, tightly covered, until ready to use. I have found that a cold batter results in a lighter, higher pudding. Here's another secret: Once you put the Yorkshire pudding in the oven, don't peek or the pudding may collapse. This recipe may be doubled.

SERVES 6

1 cup all-purpose flour

1/4 teaspoon salt

1/4 teaspoon coarsely ground pepper, plus more for topping

2 eggs

1 cup whole milk

6 teaspoons drippings from roasting pan (page 87)

In a small bowl, stir together the flour, salt, and 1/4 teaspoon pepper. In a bowl, using an electric mixer set on medium-high speed, beat the eggs until light and foamy. Beat in the milk until blended. Add the flour to the eggs and mix just until combined. Refrigerate until ready to use.

Place a 6-cup muffin tin in the oven and preheat it to 450°F. If you've just cooked the roast beef, simply increase the oven temperature and place the muffin tin in the hot oven for 3 minutes.

Remove the muffin tin from the oven. Spoon 1 teaspoon of the pan drippings into each muffin cup. Spoon the batter into the muffin cups, filling each half full. Sprinkle the tops with a bit of pepper. Bake the puddings until puffed and golden, about 15 minutes.

Remove the puddings from the oven and gently lift each one out of the pan. Serve immediately.

real creamed spinach

This is not the frozen stuff—and everyone at the table will know that the moment they taste it. The velvety texture and fresh flavor of this creamed spinach will satisfy the fussiest Christmas Day guest. Don't tell your children what it is—they might actually like it.

SERVES 6

3 pounds spinach
4 tablespoons (1/2 stick) unsalted butter
2 tablespoons finely chopped yellow onion
1 teaspoon minced garlic
1/4 cup all-purpose flour
2 cups chicken stock
1 tablespoon finely grated lemon zest
salt and freshly ground pepper

Trim the spinach of any tough stems and wash the leaves well. Shake off the excess water, then put the spinach in a large pot over medium heat. Cover and cook just until the spinach is wilted, about 4 minutes. Drain the spinach, squeeze the excess moisture from it, and chop finely; reserve.

In a skillet or sauté pan over medium heat, melt the butter. Add the onion and garlic and cook, stirring, for 1 minute. Sprinkle the flour over the onion and garlic and cook, stirring, for 3 minutes; do not let the flour brown. Pour in the stock while stirring constantly, then cook, stirring often, until the mixture thickens, about 5 minutes. Stir in the lemon zest.

Add the spinach and mix well. Cook until creamy and heated through, then season to taste with salt and pepper. Spoon into a warmed serving bowl and serve immediately.

roasted sweet potato fingers

While a classic English menu may have included roasted russet potatoes, this recipe calls for sweet potatoes, a distinctly American variety. More slender than wedges, the sweet potato fingers will be a welcome surprise for your guests, since most Americans are accustomed to eating them at autumn feasts. They're a delicious complement to the roast beef. Cook them in the oven along with the Yorkshire pudding. This recipe may be doubled.

SERVES 6

4 large, orange-fleshed sweet potatoes, scrubbed and patted dry

2 tablespoons olive oil

2 teaspoons balsamic vinegar

$1/2$ teaspoon salt, plus more to taste

$1/4$ teaspoon freshly ground pepper

Preheat the oven to 450°F.

Cut the potatoes in half lengthwise and then slice each half lengthwise into fingers about 1 inch wide. Place the potato fingers in a large bowl and toss them with the olive oil, vinegar, $1/2$ teaspoon salt, and the pepper.

Arrange the potatoes on a baking sheet in a single layer. Roast, turning once, until tender and lightly browned, about 20 minutes.

Remove from the oven, transfer to a warmed serving dish, sprinkle with more salt, and serve immediately.

peppermint stick bûche de noël

I love the fairy-tale connotations of a bûche de Noël *with its confectionery bark, berry, and mushroom adornments, and this ice cream–filled Yule log cake, which can be made up to one week ahead of time, is a fitting end to a Christmas Day dinner.*

SERVES 8 TO 10

3 tablespoons unsalted butter, melted

cake flour for dusting pan, plus 1/2 cup sifted

1/3 cup sifted unsweetened cocoa powder

1 teaspoon baking powder

1/4 teaspoon salt, plus a pinch more

4 eggs, separated

3/4 cup granulated sugar

1 teaspoon pure vanilla extract

1 quart peppermint stick ice cream, softened

Chocolate Frosting

1/2 cup (1 stick) unsalted butter, softened

1 cup confectioners' sugar, sifted, plus
   more for dusting

1/4 cup unsweetened cocoa powder

1 teaspoon pure vanilla extract

3 ounces unsweetened chocolate, melted and
   cooled slightly

Decorations

confectioners' sugar for dusting

Marzipan Mushrooms (page 95)

Sugared Cranberries (page 96)

fresh mint leaves

small evergreen boughs (optional)

Preheat the oven to 350°F.

Lightly brush a 10-by-15-inch jelly-roll pan with 1 1/2 tablespoons of the melted butter. Line the pan with parchment paper, leaving a 2-inch overhang on the short ends. Brush the parchment paper with the remaining 1 1/2 tablespoons melted butter. Dust the pan with a little cake flour and tap out the excess.

In a bowl, whisk together the 1/2 cup cake flour, the 1/3 cup cocoa powder, the baking powder, and the 1/4 teaspoon salt; reserve.

continued

In a bowl, using an electric mixer set on medium-high speed, beat the egg yolks until fluffy. Gradually, add the granulated sugar and beat until thick. Beat in the vanilla extract. Using a wooden spoon, stir in the flour mixture until blended. The dough will be very stiff.

Rinse and dry the mixer beaters. In a bowl, using the electric mixer set on medium-high speed, beat the egg whites with the pinch of salt until stiff peaks form. Using a rubber spatula, stir a few tablespoons of the beaten egg whites into the egg-and-flour mixture to lighten it. Then, one third at a time, gently fold in the remaining egg whites. Do not overmix. Spread the mixture evenly in the prepared pan.

Bake the cake until it springs back when touched gently in the center, about 12 minutes. Remove from the oven, place on a cooling rack, and let cool in the pan for a few minutes. Run a knife around the edge of the cake to loosen it from the pan. Cover the cake with a large piece of parchment paper, then with a kitchen towel. Invert the cake onto the cooling rack so the parchment paper and the towel are on the bottom. Carefully lift off the pan and remove and discard the parchment that lined the pan. When the cake is just cool enough to handle, start at one long side and, grasping the fresh parchment and the towel, roll the cake into a cylinder. Let the cake cool to room temperature.

Unroll the cooled cake slowly onto a serving platter or surface large enough to hold the entire cake flat. Invert the cooling rack onto the cake, then invert the cake and rack together and remove the parchment paper and the kitchen towel. Return the kitchen towel to the serving platter. Flip the cake back onto the serving platter. Using a spatula, spread the cake evenly with the softened ice cream. Using the towel underneath to get you started, reroll the filled cake into a cylinder. Cover loosely with plastic wrap and freeze for at least 1 hour.

To make the chocolate frosting, combine the butter, the 1 cup confectioners' sugar, and the ¼ cup cocoa powder in a bowl. Using the electric mixer set on medium-high speed, beat until fluffy. Add the vanilla extract and the melted chocolate and beat until smooth and shiny, reserve.

Remove the cake from the freezer. Using a large, serrated knife held at an angle, cut off a 1-inch piece from one end of the roll and a 2-inch piece from the other end.

Place the smaller piece on top of the log, and the larger piece alongside the log, positioning the straight edges against the cake. These are the tree limbs. Ice the cake log and tree limbs with the frosting. With the tines of a fork, draw concentric circles on the cake ends to resemble tree rings. Draw the fork along the log in lines to resemble bark. Wrap with plastic wrap and freeze overnight or for up to I week.

Remove the cake from the freezer, unwrap, and let stand for IO to I5 minutes. Once the frosting has softened a bit, use a fine-mesh sieve to lightly dust the log evenly with confectioners' sugar. Decorate the cake with the Marzipan Mushrooms, Sugared Cranberries, and mint leaves. If you wish, add small evergreen boughs, but caution your guests that these are inedible.

marzipan mushrooms

These mushrooms are much easier to make than the meringue mushrooms that traditionally decorate a bûche de Noël. Children particularly enjoy this part of assembling the cake. Let them form the mushrooms (and maybe a snowman or two) and put them on the cake. You can make the mushrooms up to one week ahead of time.

MAKES ABOUT I2 MUSHROOMS

1 package (7 ounces) marzipan
few drops fresh lemon juice, if needed
1 tablespoon unsweetened cocoa powder

Using your hands, knead the marzipan on a work surface until it becomes easy to mold. If the marzipan seems too thick, work in a drop or two of lemon juice.

Roll small pieces of marzipan into mushroom stems. Make different sizes, some thick, some tall. Roll larger pieces of marzipan into balls, then flatten and pinch to form mushroom caps. Attach the stems to the caps by pressing gently. Using a small, fine-mesh sieve, dust with the mushrooms with the cocoa powder. Arrange the mushrooms in single layers on waxed paper in a tightly covered container, and store in a cool, dry place until ready to use.

sugared cranberries

When you're not gilding your bûche de Noël *with these sweet-tart jewels, use them to garnish glasses of sparkling wine or sparkling cider or to decorate other holiday desserts. You can make the sugared cranberries up to one week in advance.*

MAKES 1 CUP

1 cup cranberries	pinch of salt
1 egg white	1 cup sugar

Bring a saucepan filled with water to a boil over high heat. Add the cranberries, reduce the heat to medium, and cook just until the cranberries begin to pop open, 3 to 5 minutes.

Drain the cranberries and pat dry with paper towels. In a small bowl, combine the egg white and salt and beat lightly with a fork until foamy. Using a pastry brush, paint the cranberries with the egg white.

Place the sugar in a shallow bowl. Add the cranberries and, using a fork, toss to coat them evenly with the sugar. Transfer to waxed paper to set, about 20 minutes. Arrange the cranberries in single layers on waxed paper in a tightly covered container, and store in a cool, dry place until ready to use.

the christmas wish book

Some time ago, I began a Christmas wish book. Over the years, it has become one of the most anticipated elements of our family celebration. In it we record our best memories of the year gone by and our wishes for the year to come. The fun part comes when you read what you wrote in past years. Did your wish come true?

Any blank book can be transformed into a Christmas wish book. Larger books weather the years better than smaller books do, and provide more space for written and visual expression.

Pass the book during a quiet time in the festivities, when your guests can take a moment to reflect. Before dinner or after dinner seems to be an optimal wishing time.

cranberry bobeches

During the nineteenth century, Americans who lived in areas in which cranberries grew enjoyed them not only at Thanksgiving but at Christmas, too. They used them as food for their tables and for decorating their homes. Now that modern shipping ensures that cranberries are available throughout the United States, everybody can enjoy the festive beauty of this fruit.

Make Christmas bobeches, or wax catchers, for taper candles by stringing cranberries as you would for a Christmas tree garland (photo page 23). Poke florist's wire through the berries until you have a string that can be formed into a circle that matches the diameter of the taper candle you will be using. Clip the wire and twist it, then fit the bobeche onto the candle, working up from the bottom. The bobeche should just touch the candlestick when the candle is inserted into it.

You can make the bobeches up to a month ahead of time and store them, wrapped well in plastic wrap, in the freezer until ready to use.

christmas crackers

Christmas crackers wrapped in colorful papers and trimmed with beads and satin ribbon are pretty additions to the Christmas table. Experiment with papers in various colors and patterns, and let whimsy guide you when you select the trinkets and candies to fill the crackers. I am fortunate to have an old-fashioned five-and-dime store in my town, and it's full of funny and clever items to fill the crackers, from nostalgic penny candies to cats-eye marbles and rings with faux gems. Party-supply stores will supply you with fitting ideas, too.

To make the crackers, cut cardboard tubing to the desired length of the finished cracker. A paper towel tube cut in half works well (each half will make one cracker). Cut the tube in half again. Using craft glue (the kind that dries clear), glue tissue paper to the exteriors of tubes, allowing 3 inches of excess paper at one end of each half. Glue another thin-gauge paper, such as gift-wrap paper, on top of the tissue paper. Make a narrow 2-inch-long tube (one that will fit snugly inside the other tube) with heavy-gauge construction paper. Wrap it in tissue and glue 1/4 inch of it inside one cracker half so most of the narrow tube is sticking out. Fill this interior tube with small candies, trinkets, and a wish or fortune written on a piece of paper. Close the cracker by fitting the halves together over the insert. Cut a wide strip of thin-gauge paper and wrap it around the cracker's seam to hide it. Glue the strip in place. Decorate the center strip by gluing beads onto it with craft glue, if desired. Trim the end papers and tie each end with a length of ribbon or twine.

Who can imagine Christmas without a tree?

Its invigorating fragrance helps to define the holiday. Its stately stature transforms a room. And decorations give it a personality that makes each tree distinctive to its own family and home.

There are many legends about the first Christmas tree, although the Germans are credited with popularizing it. During the eighteenth and nineteenth centuries in northern Europe, pine trees appeared in miracle plays as symbols of the Tree of Life in the Garden of Eden and were decorated with apples—the first ornaments!

You can celebrate this longstanding tradition with a tree-trimming party. This is the type of gathering that works with a small or a large group—family, friends, neighbors—and that is enjoyed by people of all ages. We host ours on a Sunday afternoon in December. Some guests stop by only briefly for a jovial greeting and a quick drink. Others settle in for the afternoon, heads bent in relaxed conversation, interspersed with jolts of laughter. Kids and dogs are constantly underfoot.

I don't actually expect everybody to decorate our tree. Instead, I request that each guest bring an ornament, and later I donate them to a family shelter. But we do have tree-trimming activities for the children. In one part of the house, we set up a craft table and stock it for making gumdrop garlands (page 117) and whirligig ornaments (page 118), clear glass ornaments that the kids paint from the inside. These become the children's party favors.

As friends and neighbors arrive, I offer them little cups of creamy tomato soup (page 105). Served in demitasse or espresso cups, the soup "sips" are a warm welcome to guests as they come in from the cold.

I offer an hors d'oeuvre and dessert buffet on the table in the dining room. All of the foods can be prepared ahead of time and hold up beautifully. This is one of my favorite ways to entertain because it lets me spend time with my guests, with only a casual eye toward replenishing buffet platters.

Filled with little foods that can be eaten out of hand, the buffet presentation looks as delicious as the food tastes and requires little additional embellishment. Serving pieces in varying heights, along with small, colorful flower arrangements that do not inhibit guests' movements, including poinsettia blossoms floating in water-filled bowls, give the table visual appeal. Don't forget to arrange plates, napkins, and utensils, along with serving utensils, on the buffet, too.

Since the party accommodates adults and children in equal measure, the menu includes foods that appeal to both. Among them are baked Camembert cheese coated with pistachios and dried cherries (page 108), cherry tomatoes festooned with sea salt and parsley (page 106), a warm and creamy artichoke dip (page 115), and chocolate-cookie mousse cups with peppermint candy cream (page 110). You can serve the tramezzini (page 144) from the Gift Wrapping Get-Together, too. I also set bowls of fragrant clementines, the sweet little citrus fruits, and crunchy roasted almonds around the house for guests to nibble on as they chat.

A punch bowl filled with homemade eggnog (page 104) sits on a side table, and cranberry mulled cider (simply infuse your favorite cider with store-bought mulling spices and cranberry nectar) mulls things over on the stove top in the kitchen. The cider fills the house with a spicy, seasonal aroma.

As dusk falls, it's time for Christmas carols. We give guests homemade song booklets. They're filled with pages of hand-copied Christmas carols, hole-punched and bound with ribbon. The children decorated the covers. If you do not have a piano (and a

pianist), everybody can sing a cappella, or you can have your choice of orchestral or vocal accompaniment, courtesy of CDs, or employ the talents of music students from a local college or high school.

After a rousing chorus of "The Twelve Days of Christmas," in which the group is divided into teams (which team can sing its verse the loudest?), it's time to say good-bye. As the guests depart, each is offered a big homemade Christmas tree cookie (page 112), wrapped in cellophane and a bright red bow, with a miniature ornament tied on it. It's a sweet memento of a happy day.

homemade eggnog

What's a nog, anyway? It comes from the word **noggin,** *a small cup of liquor.* **Noggin** *also means "head," which is quite hilarious since too much of this liquor-infused libation will affect just that!*

This eggnog recipe is based on a very old one from colonial America. Folding in the whipped cream just before serving lightens the drink considerably. Traditionally, eggnog is served in punch cups, but my dad always served it in champagne flutes, which gave it an exceptionally chic personality. To make a kid-friendly version, simply omit the rum, or divide the recipe in half and add the rum to only part.

SERVES 12

6 egg yolks

1 cup superfine sugar

1 cup half-and-half

1 fifth dark rum

2 cups heavy cream

freshly grated nutmeg for garnish

In a large bowl, using a whisk or an electric mixer set on medium-high speed, beat the egg yolks until light and fluffy. Gradually add the sugar, beating until thick. Stir in the half-and-half and rum. Cover and chill for at least 4 hours.

Just before serving, in a bowl, using a whisk or an electric mixer set on medium speed, beat the cream until soft peaks form. Using a rubber spatula, fold the whipped cream into the sugar–egg yolk mixture. Ladle into glasses or cups, sprinkle with nutmeg, and serve.

creamy tomato soup sips

Creamy tomato soup always reminds me of winter days in Connecticut, where I grew up. When it was cold outside, nothing warmed us on the inside like a sip of soup. I have sparked this old-fashioned favorite with mint for its sprightly flavor as well as for its holiday green. Serving the soup in small cups gives it a new guise and makes it easy to sip, too.

SERVES 12

2 tablespoons unsalted butter

1 yellow onion, chopped

1 carrot, peeled and finely chopped

1 celery stalk with leaves, finely chopped

2 cups chicken stock

1/2 cup white wine

1 can (28 ounces) tomatoes, coarsely chopped, with juice

bouquet garni of 2 fresh thyme sprigs, 2 fresh parsley sprigs, and 1 bay leaf tied together with kitchen string

salt and freshly ground pepper

1 tablespoon fresh lemon juice

1/2 cup heavy cream

3 tablespoons chopped fresh mint, plus small sprigs for garnish

In a large saucepan or Dutch oven over medium heat, melt the butter. Add the onion, carrot, and celery and cook, stirring frequently, until soft, about 10 minutes.

Add the stock, wine, tomatoes with their juice, the bouquet garni, and salt and pepper to taste. Simmer, uncovered, for 40 minutes.

Remove the bouquet garni from the soup and discard. Working in batches, puree the soup in a blender or food processor; or use an immersion blender and puree in the pan. If using a blender or food processor, return the soup to the pan. Mix in the lemon juice and heavy cream and then stir in the chopped mint.

Gently warm the soup (do not let it boil) over medium heat. Season with salt and pepper. To serve, spoon the soup into small cups such as demitasse or espresso cups and garnish with the mint sprigs. Keep the soup warm in the saucepan over low heat on top of the stove, or on a hot plate on the buffet.

cherry tomatoes with parsley and sea salt

This is fun to serve at Christmastime because the colors are so appropriate. The tomatoes are a light offering for anyone watching his or her holiday waistline, too.

MAKES 48

48 cherry tomatoes
1/2 cup sea salt, plus more sea salt or kosher salt for serving
1/4 cup very finely chopped fresh flat-leaf parsley

Remove the stem from each cherry tomato, then cut a very thin slice off the opposite end. Discard the slices.

In a shallow bowl, mix together the 1/2 cup sea salt and the parsley. Dip the cut end of each cherry tomato into the salt mixture.

To serve, pour a thick layer of sea salt or kosher salt onto a tray. Nestle the cherry tomatoes, cut-side up, in the salt.

baked camembert with pistachio and cherry crust

When baked into a warm round of rich flavor and velvety texture, you really understand why cheese is such a miracle of nature. In this holiday rendition of a traditional hors d'oeuvre, the chopped pistachios and dried cherries not only add pleasing crunch, but also holiday color.

SERVES 12 GENEROUSLY

1 whole ripe Camembert cheese, about 1/2 pound
1/2 cup chopped dried cherries
1/2 cup chopped pistachios
toasted baguette slices or crackers

With a serrated knife, carefully remove the rind from the top of the Camembert.

In a bowl, stir together the cherries and pistachios. Sprinkle the top of the Camembert with this mixture, then pat it gently so it adheres to the cheese. Wrap well with plastic wrap and refrigerate for 1 hour.

Preheat the oven to 350°F. Unwrap the Camembert and place it on a baking sheet. Bake until warmed through and the cheese gives a bit when pressed gently in the center, about 10 minutes. Keep an eye on the cheese. If it begins to melt onto the baking sheet, remove it from the oven.

Carefully transfer to a platter. Serve with the baguette slices or crackers.

chocolate-cookie mousse cups with peppermint candy cream

Chocolate cookies give this luscious mousse another dimension of flavor and texture.
To ensure the cookies are at their crunchy best, fold them into the mousse just before serving.

SERVES 12

8 ounces bittersweet chocolate, chopped

3 tablespoons unsalted butter

2 tablespoons brewed espresso

6 eggs, separated

1/3 cup sugar

1 cup heavy cream

1 teaspoon peppermint extract

1 cup crumbled chocolate wafer cookies

Peppermint Candy Cream (facing page)

12 miniature candy canes

In the top of a double boiler set over gently simmering water, combine the chocolate and butter, and heat, stirring constantly, until melted and smooth. Stir in the espresso.

Transfer the mixture to a bowl. Add the egg yolks one at a time, beating well after each addition.

In a bowl, using an electric mixer set on medium-high speed, beat the egg whites until foamy. Add half of the sugar and continue beating until stiff peaks form. Rinse and dry the mixer beaters. In another bowl, using the electric mixer set on medium speed, combine the cream with the remaining sugar and the peppermint extract and beat until soft peaks form.

Using a rubber spatula, stir a few tablespoons of the egg whites into the chocolate to lighten it, then fold in the remaining whites gently but thoroughly. Fold in the cream. Pour the mousse into a large bowl, cover with plastic wrap, and chill until ready to serve, for at least 2 hours and up to overnight.

Just before serving, using the rubber spatula, fold the cookie crumbs into the mousse. Divide the mousse evenly among twelve ½-cup ramekins or cups. Spoon a dollop of the peppermint candy cream onto each serving and garnish with a candy cane.

Peppermint Candy Cream

This yummy cream is delicious on all manner of desserts. It will elevate a lowly slice of pound cake or a single scoop of chocolate ice cream to lovely holiday heights. To crush the peppermint candy, place it in a zippered plastic bag and hammer it with a meat pounder or the side of a soup can.

1 cup heavy cream
¼ cup confectioners' sugar
½ teaspoon peppermint extract
½ cup finely crushed peppermint candy

In a bowl, combine the cream, confectioners' sugar, and peppermint extract. Using an electric mixer set on medium-high speed or a whisk, beat until soft peaks form. Using a rubber spatula, fold in the peppermint candy.

brown sugar
christmas tree cookies

These oversized tree cookies make wonderful party favors for the tree-trimming party. They're also a thoughtful way to deliver Christmas trees to people who may not have them, like nursing-home residents. Look for oversized cookie cutters in well-stocked cookware shops.

MAKES ABOUT 15 LARGE COOKIES, EACH 8 INCHES TALL

1 cup (2 sticks) unsalted butter, softened

1 cup firmly packed golden brown sugar

1/2 cup granulated sugar

2 eggs

1 tablespoon pure vanilla extract

4 cups unbleached all-purpose flour

1 teaspoon baking powder

1 teaspoon ground cinnamon

1/2 teaspoon salt

Royal Icing (page 114)

food coloring, green and other color of choice

decorating sugar in the same colors as the
    Royal Icing

In a large bowl, using an electric mixer set on medium speed, beat together the butter and the brown and granulated sugars until light and fluffy. Add the eggs and vanilla and beat until well mixed. In a medium bowl, whisk together the flour, baking powder, cinnamon, and salt. With the mixer set on low speed, beat the flour mixture into the butter mixture. Divide the dough in half, and pat each half into a rectangle. Wrap separately in plastic wrap and chill for at least 4 hours or for up to overnight.

Preheat the oven to 350°F. Line two baking sheets with parchment paper.

Remove the dough from the refrigerator and let it stand for 10 minutes or so. (This makes it easier to roll and less apt to crack.) On a lightly floured work surface, roll out one dough rectangle 1/4 inch thick. Using an 8-inch Christmas tree cookie cutter, cut out as many trees as possible. Using a spatula, carefully transfer the cutouts to the prepared baking sheets. Repeat the process with the remaining dough.

continued

Bake the cookies, rotating the pans once midway through baking, until the edges are just beginning to brown, about 10 minutes. Transfer the cookies to wire racks to cool.

Repeat the process with the remaining dough.

To decorate the cooled trees, make the icing as directed. Put 2 cups of the icing in one bowl and the remaining 1 cup icing in a second bowl. Add green food coloring to the larger portion of icing and stir to mix well. Add another color to the smaller portion of icing and stir to mix well. Cover the second batch of icing and refrigerate until ready to use.

Using an icing spatula, spread a layer of green icing evenly over each cookie. Let the icing dry at room temperature overnight.

Use the remaining icing to make ornaments. Using a pastry bag fitted with a No. 2 plain tip, pipe dots for ornaments, or pipe a greeting on each tree. While the icing is wet, hold the cookie over a piece of waxed paper and sprinkle it generously with the decorating sugar. Let it sit for a few minutes, then shake off the excess sugar. Let dry completely, about 6 hours.

Store the cookies in single layers between sheets of waxed paper in an airtight container for up to 3 days.

Royal Icing

You can substitute meringue powder for the egg whites. Follow package directions.

MAKES ABOUT 3 CUPS

3 egg whites
5¼ cups confectioners' sugar
juice of 1 large lemon

In a large bowl, using an electric mixer set on medium-high speed, beat the egg whites until stiff, glossy peak forms. Stir in the sugar and the lemon juice. The icing should be dense but spreadable. If the icing is too thick, add a drop or two of water. If it's too thin, add more sugar.

warm artichoke dip

When I was a kid, this dip was in vogue. My mom would make it for all kinds of occasions, including holiday celebrations. Now, I like to serve it, too, because it's easy to assemble and it tastes great. The recipe makes a generous amount, which is good because everybody seems to like it. If you have any left over, which I doubt, you can freeze it for up to a month, then thaw it and reheat gently.

SERVES 12

One 15½-ounce package frozen artichoke hearts,
   thawed

1 cup mayonnaise

6 ounces mozzarella, shredded

1 cup freshly grated Parmesan cheese

1 tablespoon fresh lemon juice

pinch of cayenne pepper

salt and freshly ground pepper

paprika for sprinkling

toasted baguette slices or crackers

Preheat the oven to 350°F.

Place the chopped artichoke hearts in a large bowl. Add the mayonnaise, mozzarella, Parmesan, and lemon juice and stir to combine. Add the cayenne pepper and season to taste with salt and black pepper.

Transfer the mixture to a shallow baking dish. Bake, stirring once or twice, until hot and bubbling, about 15 minutes. Remove from the oven and sprinkle with the paprika. Serve hot with baguette slices or crackers.

Keep the artichoke dip warm on the buffet by placing it on a hot plate, or transfer it to a chafing dish.

decorating the christmas tree

What's your first memory of a Christmas tree? My childhood tree shimmered with the boatload of tinsel that my sisters and I literally threw onto it (oh, the patience of my parents!). Underneath that glittering mass were colorful bubble lights, paper chains made from red and green construction paper, and a sea of delicate glass ornaments that competed with the Popsicle stick and pipe cleaner versions we brought home from school. To this child's eyes, our tree was incredibly and magically beautiful.

Now, I have my own family, and decorating the tree remains a special part of our Christmas. Our tree is a decorative collaboration among my husband, a designer who likes things "just so" (it literally takes him days to string the lights); me, with my flock of bird ornaments; our three-year-old who seems to have inherited the tinsel-throwing gene; and our teenager, who laconically offers piercing commentary like "Dad, white lights are so lame," but who secretly enjoys the whole business. Somehow, the tree comes together in a way that defines our family perfectly.

We decorate other trees, too. The real bird's tree is outside, hung with suet balls (page 21). Inside, the children's tree (see below), decorated with candy canes, ribbon candy, and gumdrop garlands (facing page), delights young guests. A diminutive tinsel tree adorned with tiny red-and-green Lady apples stands on a table in the foyer. Rosemary topiaries, strung with white lights and hung with tiny silver balls, grace both the dinner table and the mantel.

Everybody should have a Christmas tree.

children's christmas tree

This little tree that will enchant young children. Adults will smile, too. The tree is decorated with nothing more than candy canes and ribbon candy. Foil-wrapped chocolate Santas nestle in the branches. And gumdrop garlands wrap around the fantasy.

You can vary the trimmings for the tree. Other holiday candies, decorated cookies, and popcorn garlands work well, too. If you would like to invite children to help themselves to the edible ornaments, be sure you hang them on the tree with ribbons, not hooks. For safety's sake, let children know that the garlands are not edible; the thread can be a choking hazard.

gumdrop garland

To make the gumdrop garland, you will need heavy-duty thread such as clear fishing line or dental floss, a darning needle, and a supply of gumdrops of different colors. Thread the needle with the chosen thread and securely knot the end. Insert the needle through the equator of one gumdrop and slide it onto the thread. Continue adding gumdrops, alternating colors willy-nilly, until you have filled the thread. It's easier if you work in manageable lengths (about 1 yard works well), then tie the threads together until you reach the length you desire.

whirligig ornaments

While these colorful orbs are simple to make and thus an ideal activity for children, it's the surprise at the end of the process that is really fun. You never know what the final outcome will be until you add the last color and swirl. No two of these ornaments are alike—just like children.

TO MAKE THE ORNAMENTS, YOU WILL NEED:

* clear plastic or glass ornaments with a removable top (available at craft stores)
* eyedroppers, one for each paint color
* acrylic paints in various colors
* rack or plastic cups

Remove the top of the ornament. Using an eyedropper, carefully add 1 drop of paint through the top. Swirl the paint around until it coats the inside of the ornament. Repeat the process with additional paint colors until satisfied with the result. Place the ornament on a rack or in a plastic cup and let it dry completely, about 24 hours. Replace the top on the ornament.

Note: If you're making the ornaments during the tree-trimming party, it's okay for guests to replace the top of the ornament for the trip home. Once home, remove the top and let dry as directed.

birds and fruit tree

I adore birds! Canaries and finches live with us inside, and families of quail and swallows and robins and wrens entertain us outside.

I've collected bird-themed ornaments for years. One Christmas, I was looking at the tree and it came to me that, if I were a bird, I would want to be in a tree that was laden with fruit. So, I expanded the theme to include millinery fruit, fruit ornaments, and real fruit.

To decorate the tree, first string it with little white lights, then wrap it with a garland or ribbon. In keeping with the nature theme, I use a garland of pinecones.

Hang bird ornaments, birdhouses, and fruit ornaments. To hang real fruit such as apples and pears, fold heavy-gauge florist's wire into a U shape, insert both ends through the blossom end of the fruit, and thread it to extend through the stem end. Tie the fruits onto the tree branches with the exposed wire ends. You can also settle the fruits in the tree branches.

Now, stand back and look for holes, those places that need something. Into these I nestle bird nests, some with little stuffed birds sitting in them, some with wooden or foil-wrapped eggs arranged in them.

Kids and cookie decorating were made for each other.

Why not share the fun and satisfaction of decorating Christmas cookies with your children and perhaps a few of their friends with a cookie decorating party? Ask a few adult friends to join you for assistance and camaraderie.

Depending on the age of the children involved, you can bake and decorate the cookies together, but this makes for a long day. I have found it's best to prepare the cookies beforehand and then let the kids go wild with the decorating. If you wish, you can prepare a batch of cookie dough, such as the Red-and-Green Cut-and-Bakes (page 128), and then bake the cookies as the kids decorate. When they cool, everybody can enjoy them as a midafternoon snack.

As everybody arrives, hand out personalized aprons (page 138). The aprons keep the children clean while they're decorating, then become mementos of this festive day. Christmas music is a must, too. Sing along as you spread icing and sprinkle sugar on your edible works of art.

While this is a "working" party and the kitchen ought to be set up accordingly, don't forget to add a few festive decorations. The kids will be charmed. I hang an evergreen garland around the windows and adorn it with Salt Dough Ornaments (page 20) and

small white lights. You can also set a small Christmas tree on a table or countertop in the kitchen and the kids can decorate it with cookies. In company with the Christmas music, these decorations are sure to put everybody in a Christmas-cookie-decorating mood.

Classic sugar cookies are perfect canvases. I bake them in a variety of holiday shapes and invite the children to select the "naked" cookies they'd like to embellish and adorn. If you will be flocking the cookies (see page 134) as one of the decorating techniques, you will need to ice some of the cookies the night before, too.

The sugar cookies are just one of the cookies you can make from the versatile 3-in-1 Christmas Cookie Dough recipe I share in this section (page 126). This rich, buttery dough is also used for the Red-and-Green Cut-and-Bakes that bake into rounds of marbled Christmas color, and for the Peekaboos (page 130), jam-filled sandwich cookies with tiny cutouts in their tops.

At the end of the party, gather the children's edible masterpieces and arrange them in brightly colored tissue-lined boxes for the trip home. If you have the time, you can personalize the boxes with the child's name and more Christmas decorations. Add a cookie cutter and a recipe card for the cookies. On a snowy Saturday in January, a mom will be glad she has it.

Bid farewell to your guests with party favors: White Chocolate–Cherry Christmas Fudge (page 132) tucked into simple waxed-paper bags and decorated with sprigs of evergreen or holly secured in place with a stapler. The Santa Lollipops (page 18) would also serve as fun favors.

tips for decorating with kids

✳ **Clear** a large work space for decorating, and another space for holding the finished cookies.

✳ **Protect** clothes with aprons; have plenty of clean kitchen towels on hand.

✳ **Display** the "naked" cookies on a counter and invite kids to choose the cookies they'd like to decorate.

✳ **Divide** Royal Icing (page 114), sugars, candies, confetti, and other decorations among small bowls. Depending on the number of children participating, you may want to form cookie decorating teams and fill bowls with decorations for each team to share.

✳ **Plastic knives** and **spoons** are helpful for spreading frosting and sprinkling sugar. Little ones will need supervision.

✳ Have pitchers of **drinking water** and bowls of **apple wedges** and **tangerine segments** on hand for snacking; decorating is hard work!

✳ Don't forget to corral a few adults to assist you with the **supervision**.

✳ Let children work at their own pace and according to their skill level. Remember, it's the process that's fulfilling and **fun**.

3-in-1 christmas cookie dough

This versatile recipe for Christmas cookie dough is the foundation for three distinct cookies: Sugar Cookie Cutouts, Red-and-Green Cut-and-Bakes, and Peekaboos. The recipe yields as many as six dozen cookies, depending on their size, so you can make one batch and divide it easily. The dough also freezes well for up to one month.

MAKES ENOUGH DOUGH FOR ABOUT 6 DOZEN CUTOUTS,
ABOUT 4 DOZEN CUT-AND-BAKES, AND ABOUT 30 PEEKABOOS

2 cups all-purpose flour

$1^1/_4$ teaspoons baking powder

$^1/_2$ teaspoon salt

1 cup (2 sticks) unsalted butter, softened

1 cup confectioners' sugar

2 teaspoons pure vanilla extract

2 teaspoons finely grated lemon zest

In a bowl, whisk together the flour, baking powder, and salt; reserve.

In a large bowl, combine the butter, sugar, vanilla, and lemon zest. With an electric mixer set on medium-high speed, beat until the mixture is light and fluffy. With the mixer set on low speed, add the flour mixture and beat until a smooth dough forms.

Divide the dough in half and form each half into a ball. Wrap each ball well in plastic wrap and chill until ready to use, at least 30 minutes or for up to 3 days. Let stand at room temperature for 10 minutes before proceeding with recipes.

sugar cookie cutouts

Rolled and cut sugar cookies are a Christmas classic. Experiment with the shapes and sizes you make. How about a herd of reindeer to guide Santa's sleigh? Let your imagination sing.

MAKES ABOUT 6 DOZEN COOKIES

3-in-1 Christmas Cookie Dough (facing page), at room temperature

cookie cutters in shapes of choice

Royal Icing (optional; page 114)

decorating sugars, candies, confetti, or other decorations

Preheat the oven to 350°F. Line two (or more) baking sheets with parchment paper or silicone-coated nonstick liners.

Lightly flour a work surface and a rolling pin. Place one dough ball on the work surface and pat it into a thick round. With the rolling pin, roll out the dough about 1/8 inch thick (1/4 inch thick if using the cookies as ornaments). Using cookie cutters, cut out shapes. (To make tree ornaments, poke a hole through the tip of each cutout with a wooden skewer.) With a spatula, transfer the cutouts to the baking sheets, spacing them about 1 inch apart. At this point, you can decorate the cookies with decorating sugars, candies, and confetti, pressing them lightly into the dough so that they adhere, or you can bake the cookies "naked" for decorating later.

When you have finished cutting out the first batch of cookies, gather the dough scraps into a ball, roll it out, and repeat the process. Then repeat the process with remaining dough ball.

Place the baking sheets in the oven and bake until the cookies are light brown around the edges, 10 to 12 minutes. Remove the cookies from the oven. Let them cool on the baking sheets for 2 minutes, then transfer to racks and let cool completely. (If you have poked holes in the cutouts so you can use them as ornaments, push the skewer through the holes again while the cookies are still warm to keep the holes open as they cool.)

When the cookies are completely cool, decorate with icing and sugars, confetti, and candies.

red-and-green cut-and-bakes

Food coloring gives these cookies their red and green hues. I use paste colors because they offer deeper, richer color. Be careful! Paste colors are much more concentrated than the liquid colorings. Use the tip of a toothpick to add the color to the dough.

MAKES ABOUT 4 DOZEN COOKIES

3-in-1 Christmas Cookie Dough (page 126)   Royal Icing (optional; page 114)
red and green food colorings   Confetti or candies (optional)

Preheat the oven to 350°F. Line two baking sheets with parchment paper or silicone-coated nonstick liners.

Place one dough ball in each of two bowls. Add red food coloring, a drop or two at a time, to one ball and, with your hands or a large spoon, work the coloring into the dough until it is evenly blended. Repeat this process with the green coloring and the other batch of dough.

Divide each dough color into four equal pieces (you should have eight pieces total). Form each piece into a ball. On a lightly floured work surface, alternating red and green balls, press two red balls and two green balls together to form a row. Once the pieces are stuck together, use the palms of your hands to roll the balls into a uniform log 6 inches long and 1½ to 2 inches in diameter. As you roll the dough, the red and green doughs will begin to mix together, which will eventually create the marbling for the cookies.

Transfer one dough log to a cutting board. Cut the log into ¼-inch-thick slices. (If the dough becomes squishy when you're trying to cut it, wrap it and put it in the refrigerator for about 30 minutes to firm up.) Using a spatula, transfer the cookies to the prepared baking sheets, spacing them about 1 inch apart.

Bake the cookies until they are firm, about 10 minutes. Remove from the oven, let the cookies cool on the baking sheets for 2 minutes, and then transfer them to racks and let cool completely. If you wish, decorate with the icing and confetti or candies.

peekaboos

Use miniature cookie cutters to create the "windows" in these cookies. You can also use a small, sharp knife to cut out your own designs (children should be supervised, of course).

MAKES ABOUT 30 COOKIES

3-in-1 Christmas Cookie Dough (page 126)
1/4 cup seedless jam or jelly in flavor of choice

Preheat the oven to 350°F. Line two baking sheets with parchment paper or silicone-coated nonstick liners.

Place one dough ball on a lightly floured work surface and pat it into a thick round. Roll out the dough about 1/8 inch thick. Use 21/4- to 3-inch cookie cutters to cut the cookie bottoms. Transfer the cutouts to prepared baking sheets, spacing them about 1 inch apart. Reserve the dough scraps.

Repeat the rolling and cutting process for the cookie tops, using the remaining dough ball and the same cookie cutters. Reserve the dough scraps. With the miniature cookie cutters, cut out a shape from the center of each cookie top. Discard the tiny shapes that result from the pattern cutting (or bake them along with the cookies; be watchful though, as they will be done in the blink of an eye). Transfer the cookie tops to a baking sheet.

Repeat the process with the remaining dough.

Bake the cookies until they are light brown around the edges, 10 to 12 minutes. Remove from the oven and let cool on the baking sheets for 2 minutes, then transfer to racks and let cool completely.

While the cookies are cooling, melt the jam in a small saucepan over low heat, stirring until it thins.

To assemble the cookies, spread the cookie bottoms with a thin layer of warm jam, leaving a border of about 1/4 inch around the edges. Top with the cutout tops. Peekaboo!

white chocolate–cherry christmas fudge

This classic American confection assumes a Christmas personality with white chocolate and maraschino cherries and mint leaves for decoration. You can make the fudge with the kids during the party, or you can prepare it beforehand and offer it as a party favor. This is a very sweet candy and kids love it. It's pretty, too.

MAKES 3 DOZEN SQUARES

2^1/$_2$ cups confectioners' sugar

^{3}/$_4$ cup half-and-half

^{1}/$_4$ cup (^{1}/$_2$ stick) unsalted butter, cut into
   4 equal pieces

12 ounces white chocolate, coarsely chopped

1^1/$_4$ cups dried cherries

^{1}/$_2$ teaspoon pure vanilla extract

18 maraschino cherries

2 bunches fresh mint (72 mint leaves)

Line the bottom and sides of an 8-inch square cake pan with parchment paper.

In a saucepan over medium heat, combine the confectioners' sugar and half-and-half. Add the butter and bring to a boil, stirring constantly. Once the mixture reaches a boil, stop stirring and let it cook for 5 minutes. It will be thick.

Reduce the heat to low and stir in the chocolate, whisking until smooth. Stir in the dried cherries and vanilla extract. Pour the mixture into the prepared pan. Chill until firm, about 2 hours.

Invert the pan onto a cutting board, lift off the pan, and peel off the parchment. Cut the fudge into 1-inch squares. Cut the maraschino cherries in half. Remove seventy-two mint leaves from the mint sprigs (the smaller the leaves, the better). To decorate the fudge, place a maraschino half, cut-side down, on the fudge, pressing it gently into the fudge to adhere. Place two mint leaves at the top of the cherry to resemble cherry leaves, pressing them gently into the fudge to adhere.

Store in an airtight container for up to 1 week.

decorating christmas cookies

The decorating possibilities for Christmas cookies are limited only by your—and your children's—imagination!

Decorating Supplies

MAKE SURE TO HAVE A LOT OF SUPPLIES ON HAND:

* decorating sugars in assorted colors and textures
* confetti and other candies such as Red Hots or other cinnamon candies, miniature chocolate chips, and M&Ms
* sprinkles in assorted colors

* decorating pens in assorted colors
* pastry bags and tips
* paste food colorings in assorted colors
* toothpicks
* pastry brushes

Four Fanciful Cookie-Decorating Techniques

marbling

Spread Royal Icing (page 114) on the cookie. While the icing is still wet, dip the tip of a toothpick or thin brush into a contrasting color of icing and allow the icing to drip randomly onto the cookie. Using a clean toothpick, draw out the drips of icing into lines and loops.

flocking

Flocking adds dimension and texture to decorated cookies. Spread Royal Icing (page 114) on the cookie. Let dry overnight. Using a pastry bag or a decorating pen, pipe a design onto the dried icing. While the icing is wet, sprinkle the design generously with decorating sugar (sanding sugar, with its finer texture, works very well). Let stand for 5 minutes, then shake off the excess.

cookie "paint"

Use this colorful, edible mixture as you would normal paint, applying it with thick or thin paintbrushes or your fingers. For each color of paint, mix together one egg white (or the equivalent of meringue powder) with $1/3$ cup confectioners' sugar. Add food coloring (paste colors work best; add with the tip of a toothpick) drop by drop until you reach the desired color. Add more sugar if the "paint" is too thin, or a drop or two of lemon juice if it is too thick. Paint the baked cookies, then place in a preheated 250°F oven for 5 minutes or so to let the paint set. Let cool.

cooks' tools cookies

In addition to colorful sugars and candies and the techniques that showcase them, you would be surprised at the decorating drama you can obtain from tools that lurk in your kitchen. Consider these:

* A garlic press makes wavy hair for an angel.
* A lemon zester makes tiny polka dots.
* An apple corer cuts out circles.
* A fork creates stripes.
* Tiny tartlet pans, turned upside down and pressed into dough, yield pretty designs.
* A pastry crimper makes a wavy design.

five fun ideas
for christmas cookies

cookie ornaments

To transform cookies into ornaments, simply poke holes in them with a wooden skewer before baking, and again when you remove the cookies from the oven. Thread with ribbon or twine and hang on the nearest tree.

cookie greeting cards

What's more yummy than an edible Christmas card? Using Royal Icing (page 114) and a pastry bag, write a greeting on a cookie (or two or three), put it in a cellophane bag, and tie with ribbon. To mail the cookie card, wrap it well in plastic bubble wrap. Half fill a small, sturdy box with popcorn (the real kind!), nestle the cookie in the popcorn, and then fill the box with more popcorn.

cookie place cards

Using Royal Icing (page 114) and a pastry bag, write the guest's name on the cookie. Set the cookie at the guest's table setting. Or use alphabet-shaped cookie cutters to bake the guest's name or initial.

cookies-in-milk gift wrap

Transform a milk carton into a gift box for homemade cookies. Wash an empty milk carton well. Line the carton with colorful tissue paper. Nestle the cookies in the tissue. Reseal the carton and add a bow and a gift tag. Present the gift to a teacher, a mail carrier, or anybody who deserves a touch of sweetness.

miniature cookie tree

Decorate a small Christmas tree with nothing but cookie ornaments (see above). Choose a theme such as circus animals or bells. Put the cookie tree by your front door and invite guests to help themselves.

personalized apron

Personalized aprons are both practical and thoughtful. They keep little ones clean as they work, then become a memento of a festive day.

FOR EACH APRON, YOU WILL NEED:

* 1 plain apron, white or a color
* fabric paints
* paper plates
* Christmas-themed cookie cutters or stencils
* paintbrushes
* fabric pens (optional)

Lay the apron right-side up on a work surface. Pour a little fabric paint onto a paper plate, using a different plate for each color. If using cookie cutters, dip them into the paint, place on the apron, pressing down for a moment, and then lift straight off. If using stencils, place the stencil on the apron, apply paint with a paintbrush, and lift straight off. If you wish, paint the child's name on the apron with a paintbrush, or write it on with a fabric pen. Add a Christmas greeting, if you wish.

What does a girl do when she's tired, cranky, and stretched to her limit?

She calls her girlfriends. In this case, she invites them over for an evening of convivial conversation and creative gift wrapping.

In Victorian times, when a woman's work was only in the home and life was less hectic, women began preparing for Christmas in July. They would get together to quilt, embroider, and sew for the still-distant holiday—the Victorian rendition of a girlfriend party. Today, for many of us, serious Christmas planning rarely begins before the first of December (if we're lucky), and by the middle of the month, everyone needs a stress antidote.

When my girlfriends and I get together, work becomes fun, tired bodies are re-energized, and laughter, the best remedy for anything that ails you, flows freely. That's the theory behind this gift-wrapping party.

On a Saturday evening in December, we give our husbands and children their marching orders (eat takeout and rent a DVD) and the girl kingdom reigns! It's a creative potluck if you will. We each bring our gifts for wrapping, and everybody contributes wrapping paper, ribbons, gift cards, and other decorations. I augment

this with essential supplies such as scissors, tape, rulers, staplers, and pens. It's an evening that weaves gift-wrap ideas with girl talk. It's at once silly (we giggle about life, love, and lipstick) and sensible (we wrap our gifts).

But what's a girlfriend party without food? The kitchen island holds a help-yourself supper. It's a soup-and-sandwiches menu with a stylish turn. The sandwiches are *tramezzini*, the little sandwiches that are served in bars and cafés throughout Italy. They're similar to English tea sandwiches and, in fact, legend has it that the Italians stole the idea of the diminutive sandwiches from the English. They reportedly did not like the word *sandwich*, however, and thus named theirs the more lyrical *tramezzini*.

These sandwiches are ideal for a party—light, easy to eat, and so darling in their presentation. The secret to their success is to use the freshest ingredients you can find. I offer a selection of *tramezzini* that includes grilled cheese (page 146) reminiscent of the French *croque-monsieur*, a sophisticated and healthy red radish and caviar pairing (page 144), and a robust roast beef and Roquefort (page 147). To make it even easier on yourself, purchase prepared chicken salad, tuna salad, and egg salad and use them to make the sandwiches.

In Italy, the *tramezzini* are cut into their signature triangular shapes, without crusts. You can also use cookie cutters to cut the sandwiches into stars, bells, Christmas trees, and other holiday shapes. In Italian cafés, the *tramezzini* are displayed on pedestal cake stands. This is what I do, too. Your guests will find them irresistible!

A hearty roasted butternut squash soup (page 148) simmers on the stove, and a ladle and bowls are placed nearby for guests to serve themselves. Dessert is a luscious blood orange walnut cake (page 150).

At the end of the evening, you'll be nourished in both body and soul. As your girlfriends leave carrying their bundles of beautifully wrapped gifts, tuck another gift in their arms: a jar of Winter Wind Bath Salts (page 22), with an evergreen sprig tucked in the ribbon.

radish and caviar tramezzini

For these sophisticated little jewels, you can use one of the luxurious (and expensive) black caviars—osetra, sevruga, or beluga—or you can opt for the more accessible salmon roe or tobiko caviar. All will serve you well. Pairing the green tobiko caviar with the red radish gives the sandwiches holiday color. Cut these tramezzini *into star shapes for glamorous effect. You can make these sandwiches up to six hours in advance.*

MAKES 12

6 thin slices wheat bread, crusts removed

6 tablespoons unsalted butter, softened

18 radishes, trimmed and very thinly sliced

$1/4$ cup caviar

Place the bread slices on a work surface. Spread the butter on the bread, dividing it evenly. Arrange the radish slices in an overlapping pattern on the butter. Cut the sandwiches in half on the diagonal or as you desire. Garnish with the caviar.

If you're not serving the sandwiches immediately, do not garnish them with the caviar. Instead, wrap them well in plastic wrap and refrigerate for up to 6 hours, then garnish with the caviar before serving.

grilled cheese tramezzini

*This recipe is based on a **tramezzino** I enjoyed years ago at Harry's Bar in Venice. I still think about it! Perhaps it was the view, or the dashing presence of Arrigo Cipriani, the charming owner, but it was one of the best little sandwiches I have ever tasted. At Harry's Bar, each warm triangle is wrapped in waxed paper so the elegant Italian women who nibble on the sandwiches do not soil their fingers.*

MAKES 12

¹/₂ pound Gruyère cheese, shredded, at room temperature

1 egg yolk

1 tablespoon Worcestershire sauce

1 teaspoon Dijon mustard

dash of Tabasco or other hot-pepper sauce

salt

12 thin slices white bread, crusts removed

olive oil for frying

In a bowl, stir together the cheese, egg yolk, Worcestershire sauce, mustard, Tabasco, and salt to taste.

Place six of the bread slices on a work surface. Spread the cheese mixture on the bread slices, dividing it evenly. Cover with the remaining six bread slices.

In a heavy skillet over medium-high heat, warm 3 tablespoons of the olive oil until hot. Add one or two sandwiches to the pan (do not crowd them!) and fry, turning once, until golden brown and crisp on both sides, about 7 minutes total. Remove from the pan and cover loosely with foil to keep warm. Repeat with the remaining sandwiches, adding more oil to the pan as necessary. Cut the sandwiches in half on the diagonal and serve hot.

roast beef and roquefort tramezzini

The hearty eaters in the bunch will particularly enjoy these **tramezzini.** *Roast beef and Roquefort make a great pair. You can make these sandwiches up to six hours in advance.*

MAKES 12

1/2 cup cream cheese, at room temperature

1/2 cup crumbled Roquefort or other blue cheese, at room temperature

12 thin slices pumpernickel or dark rye bread, crusts removed

1/2 cup well-drained, chopped roasted bell peppers

6 thin slices best-quality roast beef

In a small bowl, combine the cream cheese and the Roquefort and mix well.

Place six of the bread slices on a work surface. Spread the cheese mixture on the bread slices, dividing it evenly. Spread the peppers on the cheese, again dividing evenly.

Arrange a slice of roast beef on the bread (you may have to fold the larger slices to fit).

Cover with the remaining six bread slices. Cut the sandwiches in half on the diagonal or as desired.

If you're not serving the sandwiches immediately, wrap them well in plastic wrap and refrigerate for up to 6 hours.

rejuvenating roasted butternut squash soup

Nutritional characteristics of butternut squash notwithstanding, this soup has a way of restoring both the body and the spirit. It's a consequence of the soup's sunny color, lush texture, and deep flavor. You can make this soup up to one month in advance; freeze in an airtight container.

SERVES 8

1 butternut squash, about 1½ pounds, peeled, halved, seeded, and cut into 1-inch slices

3 tablespoons olive oil

2 red potatoes, peeled and quartered

2 carrots, peeled and quartered

salt and freshly ground pepper

2 tablespoons unsalted butter

2 large yellow onions, finely chopped

1 tablespoon finely minced garlic

4 cups chicken stock

1 cup half-and-half

Tabasco or other hot-pepper sauce

sour cream or crème frâiche for garnish (optional)

Preheat an oven to 400°F. Lightly grease a baking sheet with olive oil.

Place the squash slices on the baking sheet and brush with 1 tablespoon of the olive oil. Toss the potatoes and carrots with 1 tablespoon of the olive oil. Transfer the vegetables to the baking sheet with the squash. Season all the vegetables with salt and pepper.

Roast the vegetables until tender, 30 to 40 minutes. Remove from the oven and reserve.

In a large pot over medium heat, melt the butter with the remaining 1 tablespoon olive oil. Add the onions and garlic and cook, stirring, until soft, about 5 minutes. Add the roasted vegetables and chicken stock and bring to a boil. Reduce the heat to low and simmer for 15 minutes.

Working in batches, puree the soup in a food processor or blender, adding some of the half-and-half with each batch. Return to the pot and heat thoroughly over medium-low heat (do not let it boil). Adjust the seasoning with salt and pepper. Add the Tabasco to taste. Top each serving with a dollop of sour cream or crème frâiche, if desired.

blood orange walnut cake

Winter is the season for sweet, garnet red blood oranges. Here, they transform this simple cake into a celebratory dessert. For added glitz—and Christmas spirit—decorate the cake with Candied Orange Peel (page 16) and Sugared Cranberries (page 96).

SERVES 8 TO 10

1/2 cup (1 stick) unsalted butter, softened

2/3 cup granulated sugar

2 tablespoons finely grated blood orange zest

1/2 teaspoon freshly grated nutmeg

2 eggs

1 teaspoon pure vanilla extract

1 1/2 cups self-rising cake flour

1/2 cup sour cream

1/2 cup fresh blood orange juice

1 cup finely chopped walnuts

confectioners' sugar for dusting

Preheat the oven to 350°F. Line the bottom of an 8-inch round cake pan with parchment paper.

In a bowl, combine the butter, granulated sugar, blood orange zest, and nutmeg. Using an electric mixer set on medium speed, beat until light and fluffy. Add the eggs, one at a time, beating well after each addition. Beat in the vanilla extract. With the mixer on low speed, mix in the flour. Stir in the sour cream, blood orange juice, and walnuts.

Pour the mixture into the prepared pan. Bake the cake until a wooden toothpick inserted into the center comes out clean, 35 to 40 minutes. Let cool in the pan for 10 minutes, then turn out onto a rack and peel off the parchment. Let cool completely.

Turn the cake right-side up onto a platter or cake stand. Using a fine-mesh sieve, dust the cake with confectioners' sugar. (To protect the platter or cake stand from the flurry of confectioners' sugar that will descend on it, tuck pieces of waxed paper around the bottom edges of the cake before dusting. Remove the waxed paper before serving.) If you will be storing the cake, do not dust it with the confectioners' sugar. Instead, wrap it well in plastic wrap and store it at room temperature for up to 2 days. Dust the cake with the confectioners' sugar just before serving.

gift rapt

You're hosting a gift-wrap party and you have everything in line, except for a few clever gift-wrap ideas. Never fear! Here are three ideas that will make you the princess of paper. If you'll be sharing these ideas with your guests, you will want to have the supplies on hand for them.

buttons and bows

I can't resist buttons. At flea markets and tag sales, in antique shops and trim-and-fabric shops, both at home and wherever I travel, you can find me combing through button collections. So, it's fitting that one Christmas I chose buttons as my gift-wrap theme.

Any type of buttons will work. You can thread like-colored buttons on baby ribbon. You can choose one or two big buttons and use them as a detail on a finished bow. You can glue buttons on a wrapped package in the form of the recipient's name or a decoration. When you know of a particular interest of the recipient, choose buttons that reflect that. For a dog lover, I have used vintage buttons in the shapes of dogs. For a sailor, I have used sailboats and anchors. Once you begin, you'll find the possibilities are limitless.

Buttons work best when they are paired with plain papers. If you're threading buttons on ribbon, choose ribbon widths that will fit through buttonholes and fasteners without seizing. Satin baby ribbon, satin cording, and cotton seam binding work well with buttons.

For a real statement, cover an entire gift box with buttons. Using craft glue, attach them willy-nilly. This artful box will be as treasured as the gift inside.

wallpaper and trim

I spent a lot of time in paint stores when I was a kid. My mom liked this medium as a way to freshen up the interior of our house. She liked it a lot. So my dad made the trip to the paint store—a lot. But it wasn't the paint that intrigued me as much as it was the tables lined with wallpaper books. In this oasis of color and pattern, I could travel from blossoming chintz to flocked paisley to staid nautical stripes—all in at least eight color variations—in the course of flipping from beginning to end.

For gift wrapping, wallpaper lends a large degree of luxe. Break out of the Christmas motif "must do" and choose whatever patterns appeal to you. Wallpaper suppliers often have overruns and returns on hand. Ask for these. You're bound to save money. A burnisher, found in craft stores, will assist you with folding the heavy paper.

I like to pair wallpaper wrapping with decorative trims and tassels. You will find these in fabric stores. Of course, you can never go wrong with beautiful ribbon, either. Make matching gift tags with the wallpaper, too.

posy packages

Flowers are unexpected but luscious adornments on Christmas packages. Search floral supply stores and craft shops for silk, paper, and even plastic blossoms. Choose big flowers and small buds so you can vary your wrap with them. One gorgeous silk lily on a bottle of wine creates a showcase hostess gift. A cluster of pink rosebuds stapled onto a brown paper bag filled with homemade cookies transforms a kind gesture into a creative expression. Sprigs of evergreen and holly on a plaid-wrapped tie box is a handsome touch. And don't think you can't decorate your packages with live blooms. You can! All you need to do is insert the stem into a small water vial, available at floral-supply stores and craft shops. A red poinsettia blossom on hot-pink wrapping paper is a bold statement, don't you think? Don't forget the velvet ribbon!

the perfect bow

* Poof and ceremony are literally at your fingertips with this easy-to-make bow.
* Start by encircling the box and tying a simple knot. Cut the knot leaving 6-inch tails.
* Using another length of ribbon, form loops, pinching them together in the middle, until 4 to 6 loops are formed on each side. The size of your loops should be approximately half the width of the box that you are wrapping. (Yes, you may benefit from another pair of hands.)
* Holding the pinched center, put the bow on the knot you tied on the box. Use the ribbon tails to tie the bow onto the package. Pull and plump the bow loops.
* To finish the ribbon tails, fold one of the ribbon ends together vertically. Make a small diagonal cut to form an inverted V when the tail opens. Repeat with the second ribbon tail.

Snowy Day Lunch

While holiday celebrations seem to center on Christmas week, there are many days, December weekends and school vacation days among them, that present us with the luxury of unfettered time. I especially like a free day when it's snowing. The outside world takes on a magical glow, while the inside world becomes especially cozy. It's as if nature has given us the permission to slow down a bit. So do!

Fondue is the perfect centerpiece for a simple, unhurried lunch in front of the fire. I cover a coffee table with a big cloth and arrange fondue pots on ceramic tiles in the center of the table. Carafes of wine and water share the space. Place large pillows or folded blankets on the floor for cushioned seating.

Everybody gets a fondue "kit" (page 162) that includes an oversized napkin, personalized fondue forks (it's easy to lose track of them in the pot!), and a note card that explains fondue "etiquette" along with the other fondue rituals of the Swiss.

The Swiss are definitely onto a good thing. Fondue is one of the easiest dishes to make, proving that, often, simple things are best. Just be sure to use the best-quality ingredients you can find, especially the cheese.

For this lunch menu, which easily could be a supper menu, I am sharing two recipes for fondue. You can prepare one or both. If children will be joining you, the younger ones should be supervised when they're dipping, swirling, and savoring, as the fondue can be quite hot.

I think it's fun to offer *bagna cauda* (facing page), with the classic cheese fondue (page 160). From the Piedmont region in northern Italy, it is a rich and savory mixture of olive oil, butter, garlic, and anchovies. Since I can already sense the noses wrinkling, I will tell you that the anchovies enrich the *bagna cauda* without imparting a fishy flavor.

Fondue is served with vinegar-flavored accompaniments that balance its richness. The small, sweet pickles called cornichons are a must. Round out the offering with artichokes in vinaigrette, mushrooms in vinaigrette, or any other pickled vegetables you like. I purchase these already prepared at the market.

The Winter Salad with Pomegranate Dressing (page 163) introduces two more complementary flavors to the table: the bitterness of winter greens and the subtle sweetness of pomegranates.

Keep dessert simple but sumptuous with fresh pineapple drizzled with butterscotch (page 164). Along with the pineapple, offer nuggets of crystallized ginger. They are yummy—and an excellent digestive, too.

bagna cauda

*Translated literally as "hot bath," this olive oil, butter, garlic, and anchovy dip is customarily
served with raw or lightly cooked vegetables. The mixture carries a big flavor that calls for "sturdy"
vegetables. Serve it with an assortment that includes red bell pepper, broccoli, cauliflower, carrots,
and radishes. I like to add a dash of red pepper flakes to the pot. I think it "lifts" the flavor.*

SERVES 4 TO 6

3/4 cup extra-virgin olive oil

4 tablespoons (1/2 stick) unsalted butter

2 tablespoons minced garlic

12 anchovy fillets, rinsed if salted, minced

salt

dash of red pepper flakes (optional)

assorted raw or lightly cooked vegetables

In a fondue pot or small, heavy saucepan over medium heat, combine the olive oil
and butter. When the mixture is hot, add the garlic and cook, stirring, for 1 minute.
Do not allow the garlic to brown. Add the anchovies and continue to cook, mashing
the anchovies with the back of a spoon, until they form a paste. Add salt to taste
and the red pepper flakes, if using.

Place the fondue pot or saucepan over a low flame. Keep the fondue hot, but do
not let it simmer. Serve immediately with the vegetables.

classic cheese fondue

This classic recipe calls for Emmenthaler and Gruyère cheeses in equal amounts and for kirsch, an eau-de-vie made from cherries. The trick to cheese fondue is not in the making, but in the serving. Wait until everybody is ready to eat, then make the fondue and serve it immediately. If you make it ahead of time and try to keep it warm, you may end up with a solid, rather than liquid, mass of melted cheese.

SERVES 4 TO 6

1 clove garlic, halved

2¹/₂ cups dry white wine

³/₄ pound Emmenthaler cheese

³/₄ pound Gruyère cheese, shredded

1 tablespoon cornstarch

3 tablespoons kirsch

¹/₈ teaspoon freshly grated nutmeg

crusty country bread, cut into bite-size chunks

Rub the inside of a fondue pot or a small, heavy saucepan with the cut sides of the garlic clove. Add the wine to the pot and place over medium heat. Bring just to the boiling point, but do not boil.

Reduce the heat to medium-low, add both cheeses, and stir until the cheeses melt and take on a smooth and creamy consistency.

In a small bowl, combine the cornstarch and the kirsch and stir until the cornstarch dissolves. Add this mixture to the cheese mixture. Continue stirring the mixture until it begins to bubble. Stir in the nutmeg.

Place the fondue pot or saucepan over a low flame. Keep the fondue hot, but do not let it simmer. If it thickens, add a bit more wine until you reach the desired consistency.

Serve immediately with the chunks of country bread.

fondue kit

Along with an oversize napkin, a fondue party calls for personalized fondue forks and a note card that explains fondue "etiquette" and other customs associated with this Swiss classic. Incidentally, a fondue kit is a nice accompaniment to a Christmas gift of a fondue pot.

✱ To personalize the forks, use block letter stamps to ink your guests' names onto matte cotton ribbon. Tie the ribbon onto the fork.

✱ Create fondue etiquette cards on your computer and print them on card stock, or create them by hand. Here are the rules (all of which can be broken):

1 Starting from the host's right, everybody takes turns dipping and swirling.

2 The dip-swirl technique involves dipping the bread, vegetable, or fruit piece, then swirling it over the pot to enable the excess fondue to drip back in.

3 When eating your just-dipped bread, vegetable, or fruit, do not let the fork touch your mouth. This results in double dipping, a no-no in fondue dining.

4 Wine, not water, is the traditional accompaniment to fondue. Water purportedly causes the melted cheese to congeal into an indigestible ball in your stomach. True? Maybe not, but why bother testing it?

5 If a woman drops food into the fondue, she must kiss all the men at the table.

6 If a man drops food into the fondue, he must supply another bottle of wine for the table.

7 The oldest person at the table gets to eat the crusty, congealed cheese at the bottom of the fondue pot. Called *la religieuse*, this is considered a delicacy in fondue circles. No, really.

✱ Glue magnets onto the back of the etiquette cards to transform them into mementos for guests to take home and hang on their refrigerators. Then pack all the elements of the kit into a cheese box. Call your local cheese shop or market and ask nicely for the boxes. If boxes are not possible, small baskets work, too.

winter salad with pomegranate dressing

In this salad, I use bitter greens because their flavor is a nice counterpoint to the richness of the fondue. However, feel free to select whatever greens you prefer, particularly if children are joining you for lunch. Winter can be tough on produce departments in many areas of the country, so seek out what looks and tastes good at the market.

SERVES 4 TO 6

Pomegranate Dressing

1 pomegranate

2 tablespoons balsamic vinegar

1 tablespoon red wine vinegar

1/3 cup extra-virgin olive oil

salt and freshly ground pepper

1 small head radicchio, torn into bite-size pieces

2 Belgian endives, sliced on the diagonal into strips

2 handfuls escarole or other chicory leaves, torn into bite-size pieces

To extract the seeds from the pomegranate, cut it in half through the equator (not through the stem). Wearing an apron to protect your clothes (pomegranate juice stains), firmly smack the cut side of the pomegranate on a work surface. (If you're working on a porous surface such as marble or wood, cover it with waxed paper before smacking the pomegranate.) Most of the seeds will pop out. (Use a small spoon or a melon baller to remove the rest.) Put the seeds and any juice in a bowl; reserve.

In a large salad bowl, whisk together the balsamic and red wine vinegars. Add the olive oil in a thin, steady stream while whisking constantly. Stir in the pomegranate seeds and accumulated juice. Season to taste with salt and pepper.

Wash and dry the salad greens. Add them to the bowl with the salad dressing and toss to coat evenly.

fresh pineapple with butterscotch drizzle

Fresh pineapple, with its sweet-tart flavor and tropical aroma, is just the thing to serve on a cold winter day. It's particularly nice after a rich meal—like fondue. You can offer the pineapple on its own, without embellishment, but it also is lovely with a drizzle of the butterscotch sauce.

SERVES 4 TO 6

1 pineapple

Butterscotch Sauce

3/4 cup heavy cream
6 tablespoons (3/4 stick) unsalted butter, cut into pieces
3/4 cup firmly packed dark brown sugar
1 teaspoon fresh lemon juice
pinch of salt
crystallized ginger for serving (optional)

To prepare the pineapple, cut off the leafy top, then cut the fruit lengthwise to yield four wedges. Using a small, sharp knife, remove the woody core from each wedge. Remove the fruit from the skin by cutting carefully between the two. Cut each wedge crosswise into 1/2-inch-thick slices. Reserve.

To make the sauce, in a small saucepan over medium-low heat, combine the cream and the butter. Heat, stirring, until the butter melts. Add the brown sugar, lemon juice, and salt and cook, stirring, until the mixture thickens, 5 to 8 minutes more.

To serve, arrange the pineapple slices on a platter or on individual plates. If serving the pineapple on a platter, pass the sauce at the table. If serving the pineapple on individual plates, drizzle with the sauce before serving. Pass the crystallized ginger at the table, too, if you wish, to eat along with the pineapple.

index